# BOUNDARIES
*in Dating*

## Resources by Henry Cloud and John Townsend

*Boundaries*
*Boundaries Workbook*
*Boundaries* audio
*Boundaries* video curriculum
*Boundaries in Dating*
*Boundaries in Dating Workbook*
*Boundaries in Dating* audio
*Boundaries in Dating* video curriculum
*Boundaries in Marriage*
*Boundaries in Marriage Workbook*
*Boundaries in Marriage* audio
*Boundaries with Kids*
*Boundaries with Kids Workbook*
*Boundaries with Kids* audio
*Changes That Heal* (Cloud)
*Changes That Heal Workbook* (Cloud)
*Changes That Heal* audio (Cloud)
*Hiding from Love* (Townsend)
*The Mom Factor*
*The Mom Factor Workbook*
*The Mom Factor* audio
*Raising Great Kids*
*Raising Great Kids for Parents of Preschoolers* curriculum
*Raising Great Kids Workbook for Parents of Preschoolers*
*Raising Great Kids Workbook for Parents of School-Age Children*
*Raising Great Kids Workbook for Parents of Teenagers*
*Raising Great Kids* audio
*Safe People*
*Safe People Workbook*
*Safe People* audio
*Twelve "Christian" Beliefs That Can Drive You Crazy*

Making Dating Work

# BOUNDARIES
## in Dating

## LEADER'S GUIDE

# Dr. Henry Cloud & Dr. John Townsend
# with Lisa Guest

ZondervanPublishingHouse

*Grand Rapids, Michigan*

*A Division of HarperCollinsPublishers*

*Boundaries in Dating Leader's Guide*
Copyright © 2001 by Henry Cloud and John Townsend

Requests for information should be addressed to:

ZondervanPublishingHouse
*Grand Rapids, Michigan 49530*

ISBN 0-310-23874-9

Published in association with Yates & Greer, LLP, Literary Agent, Orange, CA.

*Interior design by Robert Monacelli*

Printed in the United States of America

01 02 03 04 05 /❖ VG/ 10 9 8 7 6 5 4 3 2 1

*To singles who care about spiritual growth enough to do the hard work,*
*may God bless you in all you are doing*
*and make your dating especially fruitful*

—H.C.


*To all singles who want to make dating work God's way*

—J.T.

# CONTENTS

# WHY YOU DON'T HAVE TO KISS DATING GOOD-BYE

*D*r. Cloud, what is the biblical position on dating?" At first, I thought I had misheard the question. But the same question kept coming up around the country whenever I spoke to singles. We don't believe the Bible gives a position on dating. It's an activity a lot of people engage in, yet, as with a lot of other things, the Bible does not talk about it. What the Bible does talk about is being a loving, honest, growing person in whatever you do. So we would say that the biblical position on dating has much more to do with the person you are and are becoming than on whether or not you date. The biblical position on dating would be to date in a holy way.

This question about dating was asked in part in response to a movement that suggests all people should give up dating. We certainly understand the reasons behind the movement. Pain, disillusionment, and detrimental effects to one's spiritual life are three valid reasons for giving up on dating. But we don't think dating is the problem; we think people are. In the same way that cars don't kill people, but drunk drivers do, dating does not hurt people, but dating in out-of-control ways does.

The underlying issue is often the lack of appropriate structure within, among other things, a person's character, support system, values, and relationship with God. In other words, a lack of *boundaries*—and that is a character issue, a people problem. And the lack of appropriate structure, the lack of boundaries, is a maturity problem. So saying that dating is bad because people get hurt is a little like saying that because there are car accidents, no one should drive.

Avoiding dating isn't the way to cure the problems encountered in dating. The cure is the same as the Bible's cure for all of life's problems, and that is *spiritual growth leading to maturity*. Learning how to love, follow God, be honest and responsible, treat others as you want to be treated, develop self-control, and build a fulfilling life will ensure better dating.

We think dating can be a very good experience. Consider now a few of the benefits we see in dating:

1. Dating gives people the opportunity to learn about themselves, others, and relationships in a safe context.
2. Dating provides a context to work through issues.
3. Dating helps build relationship skills.
4. Dating can heal and repair.
5. Dating is relational and has value in and of itself.
6. Dating lets someone learn what he or she likes in the opposite sex.
7. Dating gives a context to learn sexual self-control and other delay of gratification.

Dating done poorly can lead to hurt and pain. Dating done well can lead to wonderful fruits in the life of the teen and the single adult. If you take this series seriously, seek God as deeply as you know how, establish a healthy community of friends to support you in the process, and keep God's boundaries for living a fulfilled but holy life, then dating can be something wonderful indeed.

For dating to be a great time of life, it must be balanced with God's boundaries of what is good. We hope *Boundaries in Dating* helps you find that safety, fulfillment, growth, and freedom.

There are many people who have been integral in the production of this material. We would like to thank Lisa Guest, especially, for all her diligent work and for the care she brings for God and the ones who use these materials. Lisa approaches our material with a deep sense of understanding and commitment to the finished work. Thanks also to Sealy Yates, our agent; the great staff of Zondervan; and the many singles whose feedback helped us in our thinking.

HENRY CLOUD, PH.D.
JOHN TOWNSEND, PH.D.

# Laying the Foundation

## EACH *BOUNDARIES IN DATING* KIT CONTAINS

- *Boundaries in Dating*—Dr. Henry Cloud and Dr. John Townsend's book *Boundaries in Dating* is designed to help singles of all ages date well. These skilled counselors and award-winning authors boldly address such issues as whom to date, what boundaries to set and maintain, and how to solve dating problems. When singles learn from the principles shared here, seek God as deeply as they know how, and establish a healthy community of friends to support them as they date, then dating within God's boundaries of what is good can be a great time of life. This video curriculum can help singles find that same safety, fulfillment, growth, and freedom.

- *Boundaries in Dating Video*—This ten-part video features the wisdom and insights of Drs. Cloud and Townsend. Interspersed are helpful real-life testimonials and vignettes from the world of dating.

- *Boundaries in Dating Leader's Guide*—This comprehensive, user-friendly guide provides all the information you need to lead your group through the ten sessions of this course.

- *Boundaries in Dating Participant's Guide*—This guide provides valuable notes and practical exercises ("Let's Talk" discussion starters, "On Your Own" opportunities to consider where you can be growing, "Boundary Building" assignments, etc.) that will help participants apply the dating principles they learn.

Additional kits and copies of the Participant's Guide are available from:

Zondervan Publishing House
5300 Patterson Avenue SE
Grand Rapids, MI 49530
Phone 1-800-727-3480

## HOW THIS LEADER'S GUIDE IS ORGANIZED

The *Boundaries in Dating* course is divided into ten sessions ranging in length from 50–55 minutes. This guide walks you through each session to help you prepare. You will also rely on this guide during the sessions, when you'll find the pages reprinted from the Participant's Guide very helpful.

For each session, *the leader* will need:

*Leader's Guide*
*Boundaries in Dating* by Dr. Henry Cloud and Dr. John Townsend

Video player, monitor, stand, extension cord, etc.
Videotape

For each session, *the participants* will need:

Participant's Guide
Pen or pencil

You may want to encourage your group members to purchase a copy (or have copies available for them to purchase) of *Boundaries in Dating* and the *Boundaries in Dating Workbook,* both by Dr. Henry Cloud and Dr. John Townsend.

Each session is divided into the following four parts:

## *Before You Lead*

**Key Points** is a list of the session's main ideas.

The **Synopsis** is a more detailed overview of the session's main points.

**Recommended Reading** encourages you to read the corresponding chapter(s) of Dr. Cloud and Dr. Townsend's book *Boundaries in Dating* in preparation for each session.

The **Introduction** includes calling the class together, welcoming them, opening in prayer, and building a bridge between the preceding lesson and the one about to begin.

## *Discovery*

Most of the session material is found on the left-hand pages of the Leader's Guide. You may want to read the shaded sections word for word, or you might prefer to highlight the key words and phrases and ad-lib. Get to know the participants and let them get to know you a little. Make your teaching personal.

On each facing right-hand page is a copy of the corresponding Participant's Guide page(s). There is also space on those right-hand pages for you to write in any additional planning notes. Having the corresponding Participant's Guide page in front of you allows you to view the page the participants are seeing as you talk without having to hold two books at the same time. It also lets you know where the participants are in their book when someone asks a question.

The Discovery section also includes the following key typographical elements:

1.  The leader's narrative is shown in standard typeface.

2.  Directions to the instructor are shown in boxed and shaded areas. These directions are not meant to be spoken.

3.  Occasionally you'll find statements you should read verbatim under the header "A Few More Thoughts On . . ." These statements (set off with a special bullet) correlate to statements also included in the Participant's Guide. Words shown in ALL CAPITAL LETTERS are words the participants need to fill in the blanks found on the corresponding pages in their Participant's Guide.

➔ Fear of INTIMACY can attract you to detached people.

Each session has two corresponding Video Segments. The video portion of the session will provide a springboard for class discussion and activities.

## Exercises

**Exercises** will be done either alone ("On Your Own"), with one other person or in small groups ("Let's Talk"), or with the group as a whole. Directions are included for each exercise. (These directions are also included in the Participant's Guide.) At the end of each session, participants will find a "Boundary Building" assignment that encourages them to begin to apply what they've learned.

## Summary

Each session closes with a brief review and a prayer.

# A NOTE ABOUT TIMING

Depending on your particular setting, you can lengthen or shorten each session to accommodate your specific needs. Be aware that discussion times may run longer or shorter than what you plan. So try to have an alternate plan for each session: know where you can cut time or add an additional discussion question or two. If you have as much as 90 minutes with your group, don't be limited by the suggested time constraints. Whatever your situation, use those times only as a general guideline.

# FIVE TIPS FOR LEADING GROUP DISCUSSION

1. Allow group members to participate at their own comfort level. Not everyone needs to answer every question.
2. Ask questions with interest and warmth and then listen carefully to individual responses. Remember: No answer is insignificant. Encourage and affirm each person's participation.
3. Be flexible. Reword questions if necessary. Take the liberty of adding or deleting questions to accommodate the needs of your group members.
4. Allow for (and expect) differences of opinion and experience.
5. DO NOT BE AFRAID OF SILENCE! Allow people time to think—don't panic! Sometimes ten seconds of silence seems like an eternity. Some of this material is difficult to process. Allow people time to digest the question and then respond.

# *Session One*
# Why Boundaries in Dating?

## BEFORE YOU LEAD

### *Key Points*

- Many of the struggles people experience in dating are caused by some problem in the areas of freedom and responsibility. By *freedom,* we mean your ability to make choices based on your values, rather than choosing out of fear, guilt, or need. By *responsibility*, we mean your ability to execute your tasks in keeping the relationship healthy and loving, as well as being able to say no to things for which you shouldn't be responsible.
- Dating can be a great time of life, but it must be balanced with God's boundaries of what is good.
- Boundaries are your "property lines" which define and protect you and your emotions, values, behaviors, and attitudes.
- Boundaries serve two important functions. First, they *define* us. Boundaries show what we are and are not; what we agree and disagree with; what we love and hate. The second function of boundaries is that they *protect* us. Boundaries keep good things in and bad things out.
- Good boundaries will help you choose better quality people because they help you become a better person.

### *Synopsis*

Dr. Henry Cloud and Dr. John Townsend don't think you need to kiss dating good-bye. Dating has its problems, but those problems point not to a problem with dating, but to a problem with people. Learning how to love, follow God, be honest and responsible, treat others as you would want to be treated, develop self-control, and build a fulfilling life will ensure better dating.

This series addresses dating problems by looking at the lack of appropriate structure within, among other things, a person's character, support system, values, and relationship with God. In other words, a lack of boundaries. You'll learn about the boundaries that will cure dating problems and even help you experience the following benefits of dating.

1. Dating gives people the opportunity to learn about themselves, others, and relationships in a safe context.
2. Dating provides a context to work through issues.
3. Dating helps build relationship skills.
4. Dating can heal and repair.
5. Dating is relational and has value in and of itself.
6. Dating lets someone learn what he or she likes in the opposite sex.
7. Dating gives a context to learn sexual self-control and other delay of gratification.

Dating can be a great time of life, but it must be balanced with God's boundaries of what is good. When dating is done well, it can lead to wonderful fruits in the life of the teen and the single adult. If you take this series seriously, seek God as deeply as you know how, establish a healthy community of friends to support you in the process, and keep God's boundaries for living a fulfilled but holy life, then dating can be something wonderful indeed.

But all too often dating means struggling, and those struggles are caused by some problem in the areas of freedom and responsibility. *Freedom* is the ability to make choices based on your values rather than choosing out of fear, guilt, or need. Free people make commitments because they feel it's the right thing to do, and they are wholehearted about it. *Responsibility* is your ability to execute your tasks in keeping the relationship healthy and loving, as well as being able to say no to things for which you shouldn't be responsible. Responsible people shoulder their part of the dating relationship, but they don't tolerate harmful or inappropriate behavior.

Healthy boundaries are the key to preserving freedom, responsibility, and, ultimately, love in your dating life. Simply put, a boundary is a property line. Just as a physical fence marks out where your yard ends and your neighbor's begins, a personal boundary distinguishes what is your emotional or personal property and what belongs to someone else. When another person tries to control you, tries to get too close to you, or asks you to do something you don't think is right, your boundary has been crossed.

Boundaries serve two important functions. First, they *define* us. Boundaries show what we are and are not; what we agree and disagree with; what we love and hate. God has many clear boundaries. He loves the world; he loves cheerful givers. He hates haughty eyes and a lying tongue. As people made in his image, we are to be honest and truthful about what we are and are not. The second function of boundaries is that they *protect* us. Boundaries keep good things in and bad things out. When we don't have clear limits, we can expose ourselves to unhealthy and destructive influences and people. Boundaries protect by letting others know what you will and will not tolerate.

Boundaries are fences protecting your property. In dating, your property is your own soul. Boundaries surround the life God has given you to maintain and mature, so that you can become the person he created you to be. You and only you are responsible for what's inside your boundaries—things like your love, your emotions, your values, your behaviors, and your attitudes. Boundaries are the key to keeping your soul safe, protected, and growing. Remember that you are not being mean when you say no. Instead, you may be saving yourself or even the relationship from harm.

## Recommended Reading

"Why Dating?" and "Why Boundaries in Dating?" the preface and chapter 1 of *Boundaries in Dating*

# Session One

# Why Boundaries in Dating?

## 3 MINUTES  INTRODUCTION

### 1 minute  Welcome

> Call the group together and welcome the participants to Session 1 of the *Boundaries in Dating* course: "Why Boundaries in Dating?"
> Introduce yourself: Tell the group your name, a little about yourself, and why you are excited about leading this course.

### 1 minute  Opening Prayer

Heavenly Father, thank you for each person who has gathered here. I'm encouraged by their desire to learn how you would have us date, and I am excited about what you have for each of us to learn. Jesus, we look to you to be our Guide and our Teacher each step of the way. And may your Spirit open our hearts to your life-changing truth. In Jesus' name. Amen.

### 1 minute  Overview

> Participant's Guide page 11.
> Note: On each facing right-hand page is a copy of the corresponding Participant's Guide page(s).

In these ten sessions, we are going to look at boundaries in dating. This course is designed to encourage the kind of spiritual and emotional growth and character development that enables dating—within God's boundaries—to be spiritually fulfilling, growth-producing, and

# PLANNING NOTES

_____

_____

_____

_____

_____

_____

_____

_____

_____

_____

_____

_____

---

*Session One*

# Why Boundaries in Dating?

## OVERVIEW

In this session you will

- Consider patterns of unhealthy dating and benefits of healthy dating.
- Define what boundaries are—and why they are important.
- Find out what you are responsible for within your boundaries.
- Begin to see how boundaries function in a healthy dating relationship.

11

---

_____

_____

_____

_____

_____

_____

_____

_____

_____

_____

_____

_____

_____

fun. These sessions are based on Dr. Henry Cloud and Dr. John Townsend's best-selling book *Boundaries in Dating: Making Dating Work.*

> Hold up the book. At this point you may wish to offer this book as an additional resource or simply mention where a copy can be obtained.

Let's turn to page 11.

➜ Today we'll consider patterns characteristic of unhealthy dating and then benefits that come with healthy dating. We'll also define what boundaries are and why they're important. You'll find out what you are responsible for within your boundaries, and you'll begin to discover how boundaries function in a healthy dating relationship.

# 48 MINUTES  DISCOVERY

## 8 minutes    Video Segment 1: "Dating: People Problems and Potential Benefits"

In the opening of this first video segment, you'll hear from people who are experiencing less than healthy dating relationships—and you'll probably be able to identify with some of them! But before I start the video, let me tell you a little bit about your Participant's Guide. During our ten sessions, we'll discuss various topics as a large group. You will also meet together in small groups, talk one-on-one to a person next to you, and sometimes work alone on an exercise. The Participant's Guide will help you stay focused and keep us moving through the material.

Turn to page 12 and you'll see that the authors have listed the key points from the video segment so you don't have to take notes while you're watching. You can use these later to review what was covered. First we'll hear some comments from people who are dating—and then we'll hear from Dr. Cloud and Dr. Townsend.

> View Video Segment 1: "Dating: People Problems and Potential Benefits."

Sounds exciting, doesn't it? Let's take a closer look at those benefits of dating Dr. Cloud outlined for us. It will be good to have those in mind as we consider the sometimes hard work of developing and maintaining healthy boundaries in dating. Please turn to page 13.

# PLANNING NOTES

_____

_____

_____

_____

_____

_____

_____

_____

_____

_____

_____

_____

_____

_____

_____

_____

_____

_____

_____

_____

_____

_____

_____

_____

_____

_____

_____

---

**Session One**

## Why Boundaries in Dating?

### OVERVIEW

In this session you will

- Consider patterns of unhealthy dating and benefits of healthy dating.
- Define what boundaries are—and why they are important.
- Find out what you are responsible for within your boundaries.
- Begin to see how boundaries function in a healthy dating relationship.

11

---

12                    *Boundaries in Dating Paticipant's Guide*

### VIDEO SEGMENT

#### *Dating: People Problems and Potential Benefits*

- You probably don't need to kiss dating good-bye. Dating has its problems, but these problems point not to a problem with dating, but to a problem with people and their immaturity.
- Learning how to love, follow God, be honest and responsible, treat others as you would want to be treated, develop self-control, and build a fulfilling life will ensure better dating.
- Dr. Cloud and Dr. Townsend will address problems in dating by looking at the lack of appropriate structure within, among other things, a person's character, support system, values, and relationship with God. In other words, a lack of boundaries.
- Dating can be a great time of life, but it must be balanced with God's boundaries of what is good.
- If you take this series seriously, seek God as deeply as you know how, establish a healthy community of friends to support you in the process, and keep God's boundaries for living a fulfilled but holy life, then dating can be something wonderful indeed.

## 10 minutes       On Your Own: Benefits of Dating

> Participant's Guide page 13.

### Directions

We will be doing this exercise on our own. Take 10 minutes to begin answering the questions on pages 13–15 and reflect on the benefits of dating you've already experienced or that you hope to experience. Afterwards, we'll look at another video segment and discover what boundaries are. Any questions?

> Let the participants know when there is 1 minute remaining. Call the group back together after 10 minutes.

## 7 minutes       Video Segment 2: "Freedom, Responsibility, and Boundaries"

Having thought about the benefits of healthy dating, let's look at three key factors in dating that result in health, growth, and fun.

> View Video Segment 2: "Freedom, Responsibility, and Boundaries."

> Remind the participants that key points from the video segment can be found on page 16 of the Participant's Guide if they would like to review them at a later time.

## 15 minutes      Let's Talk: Freedom and Responsibility

> Participant's Guide page 17.

Drs. Cloud and Townsend just defined three key concepts. Let's take some time to talk together about how the first two of those concepts are lived out in relationships, specifically in dating relationships. Please turn to page 17.

### Directions

1. Form groups of three or four people.
2. Answer the questions within your group, giving each person in the group opportunity to share.
3. Choose a representative from your small group to share your group's ideas with the large group after the exercise is over.
4. You will have 5 minutes to complete the first set of questions and 5 minutes to complete the second set. Any questions?

## ON YOUR OWN
### *Benefits of Dating*

**DIRECTIONS**

Take 10 minutes to begin answering the questions below and reflect on the benefits of dating you've already experienced or that you hope to experience.

1. Dating gives people the opportunity to learn about themselves, others, and relationships in a safe context.
   - What have you learned—or do you expect to learn—about yourself in a dating relationship?

   - What have you learned—or do you expect to learn—about other people from dating relationships?

   - What context makes dating "safe"? (Hint: community!)

2. Dating provides a context to work through issues.
   - When have you been surprised once you moved on from an initial impression and got to know better the person you were dating? Explain.

   - What have you learned—or do you expect to learn—from dating about what you value in a person for the long-term?

3. Dating helps build relationship skills.
   - What lack of certain relationship skills have you realized as you've dated? Consider communication, vulnerability, trust, assertiveness, honesty, self-sacrifice, and listening.

   - What, if anything, has dating helped you learn about relationship or about how you function in relationship?

4. Dating can heal and repair.
   - When have you seen or experienced for yourself dating as a place of learning, healing, and growth even if that relationship didn't lead to marriage?

   - Dating is a place where good things happen in people's souls. Name one or two good things that you've experienced—or hope to experience—in dating.

5. Dating is relational and has value in and of itself.
   - Why is relationship valuable? See, for instance, Genesis 2:18, Ecclesiastes 4:9–12, Galatians 6:2, and Hebrews 10:24–25.

   - As you've dated, whom have you simply enjoyed getting to know even though the relationship didn't lead to marriage?

6. Dating lets someone learn what he or she likes in the opposite sex.
   - What we sometimes think we like is not what would really be good for us long-term, but we have to find this out. When have you seen this truth played out or perhaps experienced it yourself? Be specific about the lesson learned.

   - Dating enables people to find out what they like, what they need, what is good for them in another person, and what they did not like or need. What discoveries, if any, have you made in each of the following three categories thanks to your dating?

   What you like in another person

   What you need in another person

   What is good for you in another person

7. Dating gives a context to learn sexual self-control and other delays of gratification.
   - Why are sexual self-control and other delays of gratification essential in dating?

   - Why are sexual self-control and other delays of gratification essential in marriage?

## VIDEO SEGMENT
### *Freedom, Responsibility, and Boundaries*

- Many of the struggles people experience in dating are caused by some problem in the areas of freedom and responsibility. By freedom we mean your ability to make choices based on your values, rather than choosing out of fear, guilt, or need. By responsibility, we mean your ability to execute your tasks in keeping the relationship healthy and loving, as well as being able to say no to things for which you shouldn't be responsible.
- We believe that healthy boundaries are key to preserving freedom, responsibility, and, ultimately, love in your dating life.
- A boundary is a property line. Just as a physical fence marks where your yard ends and your neighbor's begins, a personal boundary distinguishes what is your emotional or personal property and what belongs to someone else. When another person tries to control you, tries to get too close to you, or asks you to do something you don't think is right, your boundary has been crossed.
- Boundaries serve two important functions. First, they define us. Boundaries show what we are and are not; what we agree and disagree with; what we love and hate.
- The second function of boundaries is that they protect us. Boundaries keep good things in and bad things out.
- Boundaries are fences protecting your property. In dating, your property is your own soul. You and only you are responsible for what's inside your boundaries—things like your love, your emotions, your values, your behaviors, and your attitudes.

Let the participants know when there are 5 minutes remaining, so they can move on to the second set of questions. Let them know when there is 1 minute remaining in the exercise. Call the group back together after 10 minutes.

The first concept we looked at was freedom, which is the ability to make choices based on your values, rather than choosing out of fear, guilt, or need. The first question asked you to consider a time when fear, guilt, or need motivated a choice you made in a relationship. Who would like to share an experience from their group?

Solicit answers from the groups. People might share about a time when fear of a date's suicide threats kept a person in a relationship; when guilt about being happy kept a person in an unhealthily close relationship with an unhappy and divorced parent; or when the need to feel wanted kept a person in a relationship that did not honor God.

You also talked in your groups about what problems can arise in a dating relationship if choices are made out of fear, guilt, or need rather than your values. Who would give us a real-life example?

Solicit answers from the group. People might share about the problems of not being completely honest about who they are, compromising their values, being unhappy, and getting more entrenched in an unhealthy relationship.

The second concept you discussed was responsibility, which is both the ability to execute tasks in keeping the relationship healthy and loving, and the ability to say no to things you shouldn't be responsible for. What have people in your group done to keep a relationship healthy and loving?

Solicit answers from the group. Possible answers could include sharing openly about hurts and disappointments, coming through when they say they will do something, and keeping the relationship a topic of prayer.

You also talked about the problems that can arise in a dating relationship if you're not willing to say no to things you shouldn't be responsible for, if you're not taking responsibility to speak the truth in love, or if you're not protecting love by confronting problems. Who would share a real-life example?

# PLANNING NOTES

_____

_____

_____

_____

_____

_____

_____

_____

_____

_____

_____

_____

_____

_____

_____

_____

_____

_____

_____

_____

_____

_____

_____

_____

_____

_____

_____

## LET'S TALK
### *Freedom and Responsibility*

**DIRECTIONS**

1. Form groups of three or four people.
2. Answer the questions within your group, giving each person the opportunity to share.
3. Choose a representative to share your group's ideas after the exercise is over.
4. You will have 5 minutes for the first two questions and 5 minutes for the second two.

*Freedom* is your ability to make choices based on your values, rather than choosing out of fear, guilt, or need.

1. Think about some of the choices you've recently made, ideally in a dating relationship, but perhaps in a friendship or family relationship. To what degree did fear, guilt, or need motivate your choice? What did you fear, what were you feeling guilty about, what guilt were you trying to avoid, and/or what need were you trying to meet?

2. What problems can arise in a dating relationship if you're making choices out of fear, guilt, or need rather than based on your values? Give a real-life example or two.

*Responsibility* is your ability to execute your tasks in keeping the relationship healthy and loving, as well as being able to say no to things for which you shouldn't be responsible.

3. Again, think about a recent dating experience, a friendship, or a relationship with a family member. What have you done to keep the relationship healthy and loving? Be specific about one or two tasks. Also describe an opportunity you had to say no to something for which you shouldn't be responsible. Be specific about that something, then explain why you were or weren't able to say no. What were the consequences of your action or inaction?

4. What problems can arise in a dating relationship if you're not taking responsibility to speak the truth in love, to protect love by confronting problems (Ephesians 4:15)? Give a real-life example or two.

> Solicit answers from the group. Possible answers could include not being able to tell the date how his or her constant tardiness is irritating, resulting in growing anger but not changed behavior; not expressing one's likes and dislikes and therefore regularly doing things that the date enjoyed but you didn't; or that problems (being treated disrespectfully, being pressured for sex) got worse.

Freedom and responsibility create a safe and secure environment for a couple to love, trust, explore, and deepen their experience of each other. Boundaries, the third term defined in the video, also help create safety and security. Please turn to pages 19–20 and fill in the blanks as we look at what's inside our boundaries.

> Reminder: Read the following section as it is printed so that participants can fill in the blanks on their pages with the capitalized words.

*3 minutes*        ## *A Few More Thoughts on . . . Boundaries*

> Participant's Guide pages 19–20.

### What Boundaries Define and Protect

➡ Boundaries are a fence protecting your property. In dating, your property is your own SOUL. Some of the contents of your soul—your self—that boundaries define and protect are:

- Your love: your deepest capacity to CONNECT and TRUST
- Your emotions: your need to OWN your feelings and not be CONTROLLED by someone else's feelings or behavior
- Your VALUES: your need to have your life reflect what you CARE about most deeply
- Your behaviors: your CONTROL over how you ACT in your dating relationship
- Your attitudes: your stances and OPINIONS about YOURSELF and your date

You and only you are RESPONSIBLE for what is inside your boundaries. If someone else is controlling your love, emotions, or values, they are not the problem. Your inability to SET LIMITS on their control is the problem.

## LET'S TALK
### *Freedom and Responsibility*

**DIRECTIONS**

1. Form groups of three or four people.
2. Answer the questions within your group, giving each person the opportunity to share.
3. Choose a representative to share your group's ideas after the exercise is over.
4. You will have 5 minutes for the first two questions and 5 minutes for the second two.

*Freedom* is your ability to make choices based on your values, rather than choosing out of fear, guilt, or need.

1. Think about some of the choices you've recently made, ideally in a dating relationship, but perhaps in a friendship or family relationship. To what degree did fear, guilt, or need motivate your choice? What did you fear, what were you feeling guilty about, what guilt were you trying to avoid, and/or what need were you trying to meet?

2. What problems can arise in a dating relationship if you're making choices out of fear, guilt, or need rather than based on your values? Give a real-life example or two.

*Responsibility* is your ability to execute your tasks in keeping the relationship healthy and loving, as well as being able to say no to things for which you shouldn't be responsible.

3. Again, think about a recent dating experience, a friendship, or a relationship with a family member. What have you done to keep the relationship healthy and loving? Be specific about one or two tasks. Also describe an opportunity you had to say no to something for which you shouldn't be responsible. Be specific about that something, then explain why you were or weren't able to say no. What were the consequences of your action or inaction?

4. What problems can arise in a dating relationship if you're not taking responsibility to speak the truth in love, to protect love by confronting problems (Ephesians 4:15)? Give a real-life example or two.

## A FEW MORE THOUGHTS ON...
### BOUNDARIES
#### *What Boundaries Define and Protect*

Boundaries are a fence protecting your property. In dating, your property is your own _____. Some of the contents of your soul—your self—that boundaries define and protect are:

- Your love: your deepest capacity to _____ and _____

- Your emotions: your need to _____ your feelings and not be _____ by someone else's feelings or behavior

- Your _____: your need to have your life reflect what you _____ about most deeply

- Your behaviors: your _____ over how you _____ in your dating relationship

- Your attitudes: your stances and _____ about _____ and your date

You and only you are _____ for what is inside your boundaries. If someone else is controlling your love, emotions, or values, they are not the problem. Your inability to _____ on their control is the problem.

## A FEW MORE THOUGHTS ON...
### BOUNDARIES
#### *Tools and Tips for Using and Protecting Boundaries*

Some tools available to you for setting limits and protecting your boundaries include:

- Words: telling someone _____ and being _____ about your disagreement

- The truth: bringing _____ to a problem

- Distance: allowing _____ or physical _____ between two people to protect or as a consequence for irresponsible behavior

- Other people: using supportive _____ to help keep a limit

- Consequences: _____ your limits in the relationship

Sometimes you will use boundaries to simply let your date know you better: "I am sensitive and wanted you to know that, so that we can be aware that I might get hurt easily." At other times, you may need to use boundaries to _____ a problem and _____ yourself or the relationship: "I will not go as far as you want physically, and if you continue pushing, I will not see you again." Either way, boundaries give you _____ and _____.

## Tools and Tips for Using and Protecting Boundaries

→ Some tools available to you for setting limits and protecting your boundaries include:

- Words: telling someone NO and being HONEST about your disagreement
- The truth: bringing REALITY to a problem
- Distance: allowing TIME or physical SPACE between two people to protect or as a consequence for irresponsible behavior
- Other people: using supportive FRIENDS to help keep a limit
- Consequences: ENFORCING your limits in the relationship

Sometimes you will use boundaries to simply let your date know you better: "I am sensitive and wanted you to know that, so that we can be aware that I might get hurt easily." At other times, you may need to use boundaries to CONFRONT a problem and PROTECT yourself or the relationship: "I will not go as far as you want physically, and if you continue pushing, I will not see you again." Either way, boundaries give you FREEDOM and CHOICES.

*5 minutes*

## *On Your Own: How Boundary Problems Show Themselves*

Participant's Guide page 21.

Before we end this session, let's spend some time looking at how boundary problems reveal themselves.

### Directions

There are lots of ways dating suffers when freedom and responsibility are not appropriately present. Several of them are listed on page 21.

1. Read through these points, thinking about your patterns in relationships with family and friends as well as dates.
2. Then, take a few moments to answer the questions.
3. You will have 5 minutes to complete this exercise. Any questions?

Let the participants know when there is 1 minute remaining. Call the group back together after 5 minutes.

# PLANNING NOTES

_____

_____

_____

_____

_____

_____

_____

_____

_____

_____

_____

_____

---

## A FEW MORE THOUGHTS ON...
### BOUNDARIES

### *Tools and Tips for Using and Protecting Boundaries*

Some tools available to you for setting limits and protecting your boundaries include:

- Words: telling someone _____ and being _____ about your disagreement

- The truth: bringing _____ to a problem

- Distance: allowing _____ or physical _____ between two people to protect or as a consequence for irresponsible behavior

- Other people: using supportive _____ to help keep a limit

- Consequences: _____ your limits in the relationship

Sometimes you will use boundaries to simply let your date know you better: "I am sensitive and wanted you to know that, so that we can be aware that I might get hurt easily." At other times, you may need to use boundaries to _____ a problem and _____ yourself or the relationship: "I will not go as far as you want physically, and if you continue pushing, I will not see you again." Either way, boundaries give you _____ and _____.

---

## A FEW MORE THOUGHTS ON...
### BOUNDARIES

### *Tools and Tips for Using and Protecting Boundaries*

Some tools available to you for setting limits and protecting your boundaries include:

- Words: telling someone _____ and being _____ about your disagreement

- The truth: bringing _____ to a problem

- Distance: allowing _____ or physical _____ between two people to protect or as a consequence for irresponsible behavior

- Other people: using supportive _____ to help keep a limit

- Consequences: _____ your limits in the relationship

Sometimes you will use boundaries to simply let your date know you better: "I am sensitive and wanted you to know that, so that we can be aware that I might get hurt easily." At other times, you may need to use boundaries to _____ a problem and _____ yourself or the relationship: "I will not go as far as you want physically, and if you continue pushing, I will not see you again." Either way, boundaries give you _____ and _____.

---

- **Not taking responsibility to say no.** A person with this "nice guy" attitude allows disrespect and poor treatment by a date. The person disowns the responsibility to set a limit on bad things happening to him or her.

- **Sexual impropriety.** Couples avoid taking responsibility for maintaining appropriate physical limits, or one person is the only one with the "brakes," or they ignore the deeper issues that are driving the activity.

1. Where, if at all, do you see yourself in this list? Be honest with yourself so that you can learn and grow.

2. Where has someone you've dated fit one of these nine categories? How did that behavior impact the relationship?

There are many more ways freedom and responsibility problems can result in dating misery. As you will see, understanding and applying boundaries in the right way can make a world of difference in how you approach the dating arena. In our next session, we'll look at the first and foremost boundary line of any relationship: truth.

## 2 MINUTES    SUMMARY

We've talked about three important concepts today. The first was freedom, the ability to make choices based on your values, rather than choosing out of fear, guilt, or need. The second was responsibility, the ability to both execute your tasks in keeping the relationship healthy and loving and to say no to things you shouldn't be responsible for. Freedom and responsibility create a safe and secure environment for a couple to love, trust, explore, and deepen their experience of each other.

Boundaries, the third concept we looked at, also help create safety and security. When we have healthy boundaries, we don't have to kiss dating good-bye. Instead we can enjoy some of the real benefits that dating offers. That depends, though, on how effectively we use boundaries, on how effectively we use words, the truth, distance, other people, and consequences to protect our soul. Developing and maintaining boundaries will both define and protect us and our love, our emotions, our values, our behaviors, and our attitudes. And the result of that will be dating that is spiritually fulfilling, growth-producing, and fun.

As I mentioned, next week we'll look at truth, the first and foremost boundary line of any relationship. I have a special project for you between now and then. You'll find it on page 23. The "Boundary Building" exercise there asks you to note any situations in the coming week in which you would have liked to have taken greater control of your time, energy, and resources. Also note those times when you experienced the freedom of doing what you wanted and of serving others in the ways you chose. This exercise is designed to help you become aware of the presence as well as absence of boundaries in your life. Some of you will have a chance to share your thoughts and experiences, if you choose, when we open our session next week.

Now let's close in prayer.

## 1 minute    *Closing Prayer*

Lord God, thank you for what you are showing us about dating and about boundaries. As we learn more in these next nine sessions, give us the wisdom to set good and godly boundaries in dating and in all areas of our lives. Also, give us the courage to keep those boundaries. Help each one of us stay on this path of learning and growing. In Jesus' name. Amen.

# PLANNING NOTES

---

---

---

---

---

---

---

---

---

---

---

---

---

---

---

---

## Boundary Building

Before the next session, finish going through the questions in "Benefits of Dating." Then look around at your life and your relationships, dating and otherwise. Note below any situations in which you would have liked to have taken greater control of your time, energy, and resources. Also note those times when you experienced the freedom of doing what you wanted and of serving others in the ways you chose. In the first list, you will discover in what areas boundaries are needed; in the second, you will see where setting boundaries worked for you. The goal of this series is to help you build and maintain healthy, effective boundaries.

## Suggested Reading

For more thoughts on this session's topic, read "Why Dating?" and "Why Boundaries in Dating?" the preface and chapter 1 of *Boundaries in Dating*. For a more thorough explanation of boundaries, look at chapters 1 and 2 in Dr. Cloud and Dr. Townsend's book *Boundaries: When to Say YES, When to Say NO to Take Control of Your Life*.

---

---

---

---

---

---

---

---

---

---

---

---

---

---

# Session Two

# Requiring and Embodying Truth

## BEFORE YOU LEAD

### Key Points

- Where there is deception, there is no relationship.
- When you are with someone who is deceptive, you never know what reality is.
- Six deceptions common in the world of dating are: (1) deception about your relationship, (2) deception about being friends, (3) deception about other people, (4) deception about who you are, (5) deception about facts, and (6) deception about hurt and conflict.
- Some people lie out of shame, guilt, fear of conflict or loss of love, or other fears. Other liars lie as a way of operating and deceive people for their own selfish ends.
- Spend your time and your heart on honest people. Have a zero-tolerance policy when it comes to deception. Lying should have no place in your life.
- Be light and attract light. That is the best boundary of all.

### Synopsis

Where there is deception, there is no relationship. Honesty is the bedrock of dating and marriage. Deception in the areas of finances, work performance, substance abuse, and many other topics undermines relationships. The context changes from relationship to relationship, but the lying and deception are just as destructive no matter what topic someone is lying about. The real problem is that when you are with someone who is deceptive, you never know what reality is. You are standing on ground that can shift at any moment. As one woman said, "It makes you question everything."

There are many different ways to deceive someone in the world of dating. Six of the more common ones are: deception about your relationship, deception about being friends, deception about other people, deception about who you are, deception about facts, deception about hurt and conflict.

Why do people lie and deceive one another? Some people lie out of shame, guilt, fear of conflict or loss of love, or other fears. Others lie as a way of operating and deceive people for their own selfish ends. The first type of liar is a real risk in a dating relationship; the second is a definite no-go.

Spend your time and your heart on honest people. Have a zero-tolerance policy when it comes to deception. Lying should have no place in your life. That doesn't mean if you are lied to once that the relationship has to be over—especially if the person wasn't being totally clear and direct about certain preferences or desires. Probably every human being is growing in the ability to be direct and completely vulnerable with feelings and deeper things of the heart. But make a rule: "I have to be with someone who is honest with me about what they are thinking or feeling."

But if you are two-timed, lied to about facts, with a substance abuser in denial, or otherwise deceived, we caution you about going forward in a relationship. Such lying is often indicative of a serious character problem. If, however, someone goes through a deep spiritual conversion, repentance, or turnaround, and sustains it for a significant amount of time, then you might consider trusting again.

Finally, if you don't want to be in relationship with a liar, be an honest person yourself. First, be honest with yourself. It takes some self-deception to be with a liar long-term, and if you are with one, you probably know some things about that person's character you are not facing squarely. Don't lie to yourself—and stop lying to others. Be clear and honest about everything. That doesn't mean you have to reveal all that you are thinking immediately. You don't have to talk about all of your feelings or intentions on the first date, nor do you have to bring up every little thing your date does that irritates you. But in significant areas, you must not lie or deceive. Instead, be direct and clear.

If you are a person of light, not only will people of light be drawn to you, but people of darkness will not be able to tolerate the truth you embody. If you are an honest person, you will more likely end up with an honest person. If you deceive yourself or others, deceivers will be drawn to you. Be light and attract light. That is the best boundary of all.

# Recommended Reading

"Require and Embody Truth," chapter 2 of *Boundaries in Dating*

# Session Two

# Requiring and Embodying Truth

## 10 MINUTES INTRODUCTION

**1 minute**

### Welcome

Call the group together and welcome the participants to Session 2, "Requiring and Embodying Truth."

**1 minute**

### Opening Prayer

Thank you, Lord God, that you are our Light. In you there is no deception, no half-truth, no lie. May we, your people, better reflect your light of truth in all of our relationships. Please use this session to teach, convict, and transform us so that we are able to require and embody truth in our relationships with dates as well as with family, friends, and coworkers. We pray in Jesus' name. Amen.

**8 minutes**

### Review and Overview

Participant's Guide page 25.

Last week we began talking about boundaries, those "property lines" which define and protect you and your emotions, values, behaviors, and attitudes. At the end of that session, I asked you to pay attention this week to times when boundaries served you well and to times when you were aware of the absence of boundaries. Would two or three of you like to share something you noticed this week?

Note: Be ready to share an anecdote from your own life.

Thank you for sharing. Now let's turn to page 25.

# PLANNING NOTES

_____

_____

_____

_____

_____

_____

_____

_____

_____

_____

_____

_____

*Session Two*

## Requiring and Embodying Truth

### OVERVIEW

In this session you will

- Consider the truth that where there is deception, there is no relationship.

- Look at six deceptions common in the world of dating.

- Review your options when someone is not honest with you.

- Discover some reasons why people lie and learn what to do if you are lied to.

- Be called to live in the light of honesty.

25

_____

_____

_____

_____

_____

_____

_____

_____

_____

_____

_____

_____

_____

_____

→ In today's session, we'll consider the truth that where there is deception, there is no relationship. We'll look at six deceptions common in the world of dating. We'll review your options when someone is not honest with you, discover some reasons why people lie, and learn what to do if you are lied to. Finally, we will talk about what it means to be called to live in the light of honesty.

First, let's take a look at honesty, a character trait Dr. Cloud and Dr. Townsend describe as the best boundary of all. Let's hear what they have to say.

# 42 MINUTES  DISCOVERY

## 6 minutes    *Video Segment 1: "Standing on Quicksand"*

> Remind the participants that key points of the video segment can be found on page 26 of the Participant's Guide if they would like to review them at a later time.

> View Video Segment 1: "Standing on Quicksand."

## 15 minutes   *Let's Talk: Deception in Dating*

> Participant's Guide page 27.

Maybe as you heard Dr. Cloud and Dr. Townsend talk about six forms of deception in dating, you thought about experiences with deception you've had in relationships. Now you'll have a chance to talk about those experiences and possible reasons why that deception occurred. Let's turn to page 27.

### Directions

1. I will be dividing the class into six groups and assigning each group one kind of deception to discuss.
2. Answer the questions listed for your group's type of deception, giving each person the opportunity to share.
3. Choose a representative from your small group to share your ideas after the exercise is over.
4. You'll have 5 minutes to complete this exercise. Any questions?

# PLANNING NOTES

_____

_____

_____

_____

_____

_____

_____

_____

_____

_____

_____

---

## Session Two

# Requiring and Embodying Truth

### OVERVIEW

In this session you will

- Consider the truth that where there is deception, there is no relationship.
- Look at six deceptions common in the world of dating.
- Review your options when someone is not honest with you.
- Discover some reasons why people lie and learn what to do if you are lied to.
- Be called to live in the light of honesty.

25

---

### VIDEO SEGMENT

#### Standing on Quicksand

- Where there is deception, there is no relationship.
- When you are with someone who is deceptive, you never know what reality is.
- There are many different ways to deceive someone in the world of dating:

  1. Deception about your relationship
  2. Deception about being friends
  3. Deception about other people
  4. Deception about who you are
  5. Deception about facts
  6. Deception about hurt and conflict

---

### LET'S TALK

#### Deception in Dating

**DIRECTIONS**

1. The leader will be dividing the class into six groups and assigning each group one kind of deception to discuss.
2. Answer the questions listed for your group's type of deception, giving each person the opportunity to share.
3. Choose a representative from your small group to share your ideas after the exercise is over.
4. You'll have 5 minutes to complete this exercise.

**Deception about Your Relationship**

1. When, if ever, have you been deceived about a relationship's significance to the other person involved? What did you learn from your experience?

2. When, if ever, have you deceived a person you were dating about the relationship's significance to you? What did you learn from that experience or from this discussion of such an experience?

**Deception about Being Friends**

1. When, if ever, has someone pretended to be a friend to you but had ulterior motives? What impact did that deception have on the "friendship"?

> After splitting the large group into six small groups, assign each group one type of deception. Let the participants know when there is 1 minute remaining. Call the group back together after 5 minutes.

> Note: We have allowed 10 minutes for discussion. Your review of the following questions will depend on how much time you have available.

The first group discussed **deception about your relationship**. As soon as someone is sure that dating is not going where another person thinks or hopes it is, that person has a responsibility to tell the other one clearly and honestly. Anything less is deceitful and harmful. What real-life example of being deceived (or even of being the deceiver) can someone from this group share? And what did that experience teach the person involved?

> Solicit answers from the groups. Possible answers could include being led on by a date who had just ended a longtime relationship or letting someone say "I love you" without explaining that your feelings didn't match.

The second group discussed **deception about being friends**. Some people are deceptive about their true intentions while they are acting like a friend. You shouldn't act like a friend that you're not—and only you know for sure. What can someone from this group share about a time someone pretended to be a friend but had ulterior motives? What impact did that deception have on the "friendship"? What would have been a healthier (i.e., honest) approach?

> Solicit answers from the group. Possible deception about being friends could occur in an office relationship, a ministry partnership, or a time when a person talks about a recently broken heart.

The third group talked about **deception about other people**. Sometimes people deceive each other about the nature of other people in their lives. They may act like someone is "just a friend" when there is more of a history or more in the present than is being said. Once a pattern of deception is begun, trust is difficult to reestablish. Would someone from the third group share about a time when someone was less than honest about a person in his/her life? What happened after that deception was revealed?

> Solicit answers from the group. Possible situations could include wanting to impress a former girlfriend by bringing a new date to a party she was attending or not letting a new date know that you were once in relationship with someone you have regular contact with.

# PLANNING NOTES

_____

_____

_____

_____

_____

_____

_____

_____

_____

_____

_____

---

### LET'S TALK
#### *Deception in Dating*

**DIRECTIONS**

1. The leader will be dividing the class into six groups and assigning each group one kind of deception to discuss.
2. Answer the questions listed for your group's type of deception, giving each person the opportunity to share.
3. Choose a representative from your small group to share your ideas after the exercise is over.
4. You'll have 5 minutes to complete this exercise.

#### *Deception about Your Relationship*

1. When, if ever, have you been deceived about a relationship's significance to the other person involved? What did you learn from your experience?

2. When, if ever, have you deceived a person you were dating about the relationship's significance to you? What did you learn from that experience or from this discussion of such an experience?

#### *Deception about Being Friends*

1. When, if ever, has someone pretended to be a friend to you but had ulterior motives? What impact did that deception have on the "friendship"?

---

2. When, if ever, have you pretended to be a friend but had ulterior motives? What would have been a healthier (i.e., honest) approach?

#### *Deception about Other People*

1. When, if ever, has someone you've dated been less than honest about someone in his or her life? What happened after that deception was revealed?

2. When, if ever, have you been less than honest with someone about another person in your life? What statement of the truth could you have made early on? What pain (your own or someone else's) might have been avoided had you been honest?

#### *Deception about Who You Are*

1. Why do you hesitate, if you do, to be honest about everything, from the kind of ice cream you like to what you believe about God? What does your answer tell you about yourself—and what will you do to become healthier?

2. Maybe you've known or dated someone who wasn't able to be honest, who hesitated even to express an opinion or make a choice. How did you respond? Why is such behavior bad for a relationship?

---

#### *Deception about Facts*

1. When, if ever, has someone you've known or dated lied about reality? Was that deception a red flag for you? Why or why not? Why would such deception be a red flag?

2. When, if ever, have you lied about reality to someone you've known or dated? Why did you do that? What impact did your dishonesty have on your relationship? (Or, if you've never experienced this, what impact could this kind of dishonesty have on a relationship?) What are you doing to become a person of greater integrity?

#### *Deception about Hurt and Conflict*

1. When there is a problem with how you've been treated or when you have suffered some hurt, you must be honest. When have you opted for honesty? What happened? And when, if ever, have you kept quiet instead of being honest—and what happened in the relationship?

2. How do you respond when a person is honest about how you have hurt him or her or when you're trying to resolve a conflict? How would you like to respond—and what will you do to get to that point?

> Being honest is totally up to you. What the person you are dating does you cannot control. But you can decide what kind of person you are going to be, and as a result, you will also be deciding what kind of person you are going to be with.

The fourth group discussed ***deception about who you are***. It is important to remember that you will have a good relationship to the degree that you are able to be clear and honest about everything. Dr. Cloud and Dr. Townsend remind us to "be honest with your date, have some differences, and enjoy the trip." But why do some people hesitate to be honest? Who from this group would like to share some thoughts from your group discussion?

> Possible answers could include fear of being rejected because of one's likes or dislikes; ignorance about how to voice an opinion; or being compliant in order to be liked.

Why is being unable to be honest, being unable even to express an opinion or make a choice, bad for a relationship?

> Possible answers could include: "Someone is not being totally honest — and for whatever reason doesn't feel comfortable taking that risk" or "It's hard to get to know someone who never shares ideas or preferences."

The fifth group discussed ***deception about facts***. Some people tell lies not about feelings, relationships, or personal preferences, but about reality itself, about cold, hard, objective facts. When you catch the person you are dating in any kind of lie, see that as a character issue that you should take as a very solemn warning. Who would like to share your group's thoughts about what causes people to lie about facts?

> Solicit answers from the group. Possible causes could include the desire to impress and be liked, guilt or discomfort about past mistakes, and perhaps even lying out of habit.

Finally, the sixth group discussed ***deception about hurt and conflict.*** One of the most important things you can do in a dating relationship is to be honest about hurt and conflict. Being honest about how you've been treated or when you have suffered some hurt enables you to resolve the hurt or conflict. What did someone share about when he or she chose to be honest? What happened in the relationship?

> Solicit answers from the group. Possible answers could include: "The person apologized and changed" or "The person got really angry, and I realized I didn't want to be hanging around with her."

➡ Remember: "Being honest is totally up to you. What the person you are dating does you cannot control. But you can decide what kind of person you are going to be, and as a result, you will also be deciding what kind of person you are going to be with."

# PLANNING NOTES

_____

_____

_____

_____

_____

_____

_____

_____

_____

_____

_____

_____

_____

_____

_____

_____

_____

_____

_____

_____

_____

_____

_____

_____

_____

_____

_____

_____

---

2. When, if ever, have you pretended to be a friend but had ulterior motives? What would have been a healthier (i.e., honest) approach?

### Deception about Other People

1. When, if ever, has someone you've dated been less than honest about someone in his or her life? What happened after that deception was revealed?

2. When, if ever, have you been less than honest with someone about another person in your life? What statement of the truth could you have made early on? What pain (your own or someone else's) might have been avoided had you been honest?

### Deception about Who You Are

1. Why do you hesitate, if you do, to be honest about everything, from the kind of ice cream you like to what you believe about God? What does your answer tell you about yourself—and what will you do to become healthier?

2. Maybe you've known or dated someone who wasn't able to be honest, who hesitated even to express an opinion or make a choice. How did you respond? Why is such behavior bad for a relationship?

---

### Deception about Facts

1. When, if ever, has someone you've known or dated lied about reality? Was that deception a red flag for you? Why or why not? Why would such deception be a red flag?

2. When, if ever, have you lied about reality to someone you've known or dated? Why did you do that? What impact did your dishonesty have on your relationship? (Or, if you've never experienced this, what impact could this kind of dishonesty have on a relationship?) What are you doing to become a person of greater integrity?

### Deception about Hurt and Conflict

1. When there is a problem with how you've been treated or when you have suffered some hurt, you must be honest. When have you opted for honesty? What happened? And when, if ever, have you kept quiet instead of being honest—and what happened in the relationship?

2. How do you respond when a person is honest about how you have hurt him or her or when you're trying to resolve a conflict? How would you like to respond—and what will you do to get to that point?

> Being honest is totally up to you. What the person you are dating does you cannot control. But you can decide what kind of person you are going to be, and as a result, you will also be deciding what kind of person you are going to be with.

On that note, let's hear some more from Dr. Cloud and Dr. Townsend.

**6 minutes**

## Video Segment 2: "Honesty: The Best Boundary of All"

> Remind the participants that key points from the video segment can be found on page 30 of the Participant's Guide if they would like to review them at a later time.

> View Video Segment 2: "Honesty: The Best Boundary of All."

Please turn to page 30.

**10 minutes**

## Let's Talk: Truth or Consequences?

> Participant's Guide page 31.

### Directions

Please form groups of three or four and discuss the questions listed on page 31. Be sure to allow enough time so that each member of the group has an opportunity to share. You will have 10 minutes for this exercise. Any questions?

> Let the participants know when there is 1 minute remaining. Call the group back together after 10 minutes. If you have time, repeat the questions back to the group, asking for volunteers from each of the groups to share their group's answers.

Thanks for sharing. Now it's time to drive home some of these points about honesty. Turn to page 32.

**5 minutes**

## A Few More Thoughts on ... Dealing with Deception

> Participant's Guide page 32.

➔ Don't tolerate deception or lying when it happens. Make a rule: "I have to be with someone who is honest with me about what they are thinking or feeling." But what should you do if you are lied to? Here are six steps Dr. Cloud and Dr. Townsend suggest:

---

## VIDEO SEGMENT

### *Honesty: The Best Boundary of All*

- Where there is deception, there is no relationship.

- Why do people lie? Some people lie out of shame, guilt, fear of conflict or loss of love, or other fears. Other liars lie as a way of operating and deceive people for their own selfish ends.

- Spend your time and your heart on honest people. Have a zero-tolerance policy when it comes to deception. Lying should have no place in your life.

- If you don't want to be in relationship with a liar, be an honest person yourself—honest with yourself and honest with other people.

- Be light and attract light. That is the best boundary of all.

---

## LET'S TALK

### *Truth or Consequences?*

**DIRECTIONS**

Please form groups of three or four and discuss the questions below. Be sure to allow enough time so that each member of the group has an opportunity to share. You will have 10 minutes for this exercise.

1. Trying to help someone learn to tell the truth is a noble goal. But why is the attempt to rehabilitate not appropriate in a dating relationship? And why should you run, run, run from a perpetual liar?

2. Drs. Cloud and Townsend are clear, straightforward, and unwavering: *Do not tolerate lying*, period. Nevertheless, they understand that intimacy grows in a dating relationship, and that people use a "fig leaf" to cover up sometimes. Explain in practical terms how those points don't weaken their call to not tolerate lying.

3. Why does being honest attract honest people rather than deceivers? Feel free to use Jesus' metaphor of light and darkness in your answer (John 3:19–21).

---

## A FEW MORE THOUGHTS ON ...
## DEALING WITH DECEPTION

Don't tolerate deception or lying when it happens. Make a rule: "I have to be with someone who is honest with me about what they are thinking or feeling." But what should you do if you are lied to? Here are six steps Dr. Cloud and Dr. Townsend suggest:

1. _____ the lie.

2. Hear the response and see how much _____ and _____ there is for the lying.

3. Try to figure out what the lying _____ in the relationship. If the person is afraid, guilty, or fears the loss of your love, then work on that dynamic and try to determine if the character issue is changing. But be _____.

4. Look at the level of _____ and _____. How significantly is the person pursuing _____ and _____? How internally _____ is he or she to get better?

5. Is the change being _____? Make sure you give it enough _____. Just hearing "I'm sorry" is not good enough.

6. Look at the kind of _____ it was. Was it to _____ himself or herself or just to serve _____ ends? If it is the latter, face reality squarely that you are with a person who loves himself more than the truth and face what that means. If the former, think long and hard, and have a good reason to continue in the relationship.

---

Honesty is the bedrock of any relationship. This week, be on the alert for moments when you're tempted, for whatever reason, to deceive. Make it your prayer to stand strong and be truthful. (If you notice a severe tendency to lie in order to deceive others for your own selfish ends, consider getting help.) Ask the Holy Spirit to help you be light.

## Boundary Building

- Look again at "A Few More Thoughts on... Dealing with Deception." What steps listed there would be hard for you to take? Who could help you take those steps if you ever need to?
- Review why you should deal with lying in a relationship rather than ignoring it or pretending it isn't there.
- Are you an honest person? Explain why you've answered as you have. What evidence (including people you're in relationship with) can you point to in support of your yes or no?
- This week be on the alert for moments when you're tempted, for whatever reason, to deceive. Make it your prayer to stand strong and be truthful. (If you notice a severe tendency to lie in order to deceive others for your own selfish ends, consider getting help.) Ask the Holy Spirit to help you be light.

## Suggested Reading

For more thoughts on this session's topic, read chapter 2 in *Boundaries in Dating:* "Require and Embody Truth." For a more thorough self-evaluation, look at chapter 2 in the *Boundaries in Dating Workbook.*

1. CONFRONT the lie.
2. Hear the response and see how much OWNERSHIP and SORROW there is for the lying.
3. Try to figure out what the lying MEANS in the relationship. If the person is afraid, guilty, or fears the loss of your love, then work on that dynamic and try to determine if the character issue is changing. But be CAREFUL.
4. Look at the level of REPENTANCE and CHANGE. How significantly is the person pursuing HOLINESS and PURITY? How internally MOTIVATED is he or she to get better?
5. Is the change being SUSTAINED? Make sure you give it enough TIME. Just hearing "I'm sorry" is not good enough.
6. Look at the kind of LYING it was. Was it to PROTECT himself or herself or just to serve SELFISH ends? If it is the latter, face reality squarely that you are with a person who loves himself more than the truth and face what that means. If the former, think long and hard and have a good reason to continue in the relationship.

## 2 MINUTES    SUMMARY

On page 33 you will find this week's "Boundary Building" exercise. We've talked about the fact that being honest attracts honest people rather than deceivers. This exercise will give you a chance to think about how good you are at being honest as well as how well you deal with being lied to.

Dr. Cloud and Dr. Townsend couldn't have been any clearer: honesty is the bedrock of any relationship. In fact, where there is deception, there is no relationship. This week's "Boundary Building" asks you to be alert to how honest you are in your relationships and in your day-to-day activities. It reads, "Be on the alert for moments when you're tempted, for whatever reason, to deceive. Make it your prayer to stand strong and be truthful. (If you notice a severe tendency to lie in order to deceive others for your own selfish ends, consider getting help.) Ask the Holy Spirit to help you be light."

Let's ask him together right now.

## 1 minute    *Closing Prayer*

Holy Spirit, help us to live truthfully in everything we do, in every relationship and every activity. Make us light in our relationships—and help us not to be afraid to confront darkness. Give us wisdom and boldness to deal with deception when we see it, and then give us the courage to walk away from a relationship that isn't going to be based in truth. Help us to live in the light of honesty, the light of truth, and to reflect the light of God in all we do. We pray in Jesus' name. Amen.

# PLANNING NOTES

_____

_____

_____

_____

_____

_____

_____

_____

_____

_____

_____

_____

_____

_____

_____

_____

_____

_____

_____

_____

_____

_____

---

### A FEW MORE THOUGHTS ON . . .
### DEALING WITH DECEPTION

Don't tolerate deception or lying when it happens. Make a rule: "I have to be with someone who is honest with me about what they are thinking or feeling." But what should you do if you are lied to? Here are six steps Dr. Cloud and Dr. Townsend suggest:

1. _____ the lie.

2. Hear the response and see how much _____ and _____ there is for the lying.

3. Try to figure out what the lying _____ in the relationship. If the person is afraid, guilty, or fears the loss of your love, then work on that dynamic and try to determine if the character issue is changing. But be _____.

4. Look at the level of _____ and _____. How significantly is the person pursuing _____ and _____? How internally _____ is he or she to get better?

5. Is the change being _____? Make sure you give it enough _____. Just hearing "I'm sorry" is not good enough.

6. Look at the kind of _____ it was. Was it to _____ himself or herself or just to serve _____ ends? If it is the latter, face reality squarely that you are with a person who loves himself more than the truth and face what that means. If the former, think long and hard, and have a good reason to continue in the relationship.

---

Honesty is the bedrock of any relationship. This week, be on the alert for moments when you're tempted, for whatever reason, to deceive. Make it your prayer to stand strong and be truthful. (If you notice a severe tendency to lie in order to deceive others for your own selfish ends, consider getting help.) Ask the Holy Spirit to help you be light.

## Boundary Building

- Look again at "A Few More Thoughts on . . . Dealing with Deception." What steps listed there would be hard for you to take? Who could help you take those steps if you ever need to?
- Review why you should deal with lying in a relationship rather than ignoring it or pretending it isn't there.
- Are you an honest person? Explain why you've answered as you have. What evidence (including people you're in relationship with) can you point to in support of your yes or no?
- This week be on the alert for moments when you're tempted, for whatever reason, to deceive. Make it your prayer to stand strong and be truthful. (If you notice a severe tendency to lie in order to deceive others for your own selfish ends, consider getting help.) Ask the Holy Spirit to help you be light.

## Suggested Reading

For more thoughts on this session's topic, read chapter 2 in *Boundaries in Dating:* "Require and Embody Truth." For a more thorough self-evaluation, look at chapter 2 in the *Boundaries in Dating Workbook*.

# Session Three — Taking God on a Date

## BEFORE YOU LEAD

### Key Points

- The issue is not how to fit our spiritual life into our dating life; rather, it is how to fit our dating life into our spiritual life.
- When we're dating, we desire God *and* we desire a person. And sometimes we don't know if the desires are working together or not.
- There are several aspects of your spiritual life that you will want to bring into the relationship: your faith story, values, struggles, spiritual autonomy, and friendships.
- Fall in love with someone who is passionate about matters of faith, enough to wrestle with and discuss their meaning with you. Some of the most meaningful times of growth for dates can be when they argue, read the Bible, and come to terms on spiritual matters.
- There are religious people and there are spiritual people. Religious people *know* the Truth, but spiritual people *do* it.
- Even if you do not end up marrying the person you are dating, take the stance that during your tenure as dates, you both will grow spiritually.
- Don't interpret religious agreement or passivity on your date's part as spiritual compatibility.
- Develop a relationship in which you are challenging each other to "walk your talk." And that "walking" includes the ability to love and be humble.

### Synopsis

People have varying degrees of success in taking God on a date or, more specifically, into a dating relationship. Sometimes people try to fit their spiritual life into their dating life. That's upside-down dating. The issue needs to be how to fit our dating life into our spiritual life, not vice versa. Life and love are God's gifts and fall under his domain. So the right-side-up approach is to bring dating before God and ask for his guidance. It is good to offer our dating as part of the living sacrifice that helps submit all aspects of our lives to God's order for our existence. The more our lives are surrendered to him, the more he is able to fashion our lives as they were meant to be.

Sometimes people start out strong, having Jesus Christ at the center of their relationship, their activities, and their conversation. But then they'll notice that their relationship with God waxes and wanes depending on what their date is doing with the Lord. They are excited about God when their date is doing well spiritually, but they distance themselves from the Lord and don't take responsibility for their spiritual health or growth when their date is struggling. They don't own their relationship with God for themselves. This kind of dependence on a date for the status of one's relationship with God can be a form of idolatry.

When we demand that dating bring us the love, fulfillment, or desire we want without allowing God to point the way, we can miss God's design for us, and we run the risk of going to the creation, rather than the Creator, as our ultimate source of life. Many times people will find their relationship with God taking some sort of detour as their dating world becomes more involved. Again, surrendering all of your life to God is the first and necessary step of bringing dating in line with God.

Dating right-side-up can be an enriching and exciting experience. When you find a person who challenges you spiritually, you don't always have to be the instigator—the one to provide the impetus for spiritual connection and growth.

You can share deeper parts of yourself, thereby growing closer to each other and to God. Some of those deeper parts of yourself you'll want to bring into your dating relationship are your faith story, your values, your struggles, spiritual autonomy, and friendships. It's a great experience to begin to unveil yourself to your date spiritually.

As you do open up spiritually, consider that differences can promote growth. Demanding that your date have exactly the same spiritual values as you could be a problem. You need to be in agreement on the fundamentals of the Christian faith, but you also want to be in relationship with someone who has thought through their own spiritual issues deeply and individually and has reached their own conclusions. In fact, we'll encourage you to fall in love with someone who is passionate about matters of faith enough to wrestle with and discuss their meaning with you.

Watch to see how your date integrates faith into real life. After all, there are religious people, and there are spiritual people. Religious people *know* the Truth, but spiritual people *do* it. You want yourself and your date to have lives that reflect both knowing and doing spirituality in the real world. That is what character is all about: integrating the realities of God's ordinances into the relational, financial, sexual, job concerns, and other aspects of everyday life.

Another aspect of the spiritual part of dating is that it is important to matter to each other on a spiritual level. Be part of each other's spiritual growth and conduct. Even if you do not end up marrying each other, take the stance that during your tenure as dates, you both will grow spiritually. Develop a relationship in which you are both challenging each other to "walk your talk."

# *Recommended Reading*

"Take God on a Date," chapter 3 of *Boundaries in Dating*

# Session Three

# Taking God on a Date

## 7 MINUTES    INTRODUCTION

### 3 minutes    Welcome

### 1 minute    Opening Prayer

Lord God, I thank you for these people who show by gathering here that they want to live in a way that honors you. I pray, Lord, that you have used last week's discussion to help each one of us be more honest in all that we say and do. May our honesty indeed be an effective boundary for us, and may it help us be your light in the world. I also ask you to use what you have for us today to grow us into the people you want us to be. In Jesus' name. Amen.

### 3 minutes    Review and Overview

Participant's Guide page 35.

In our first session, we defined *boundaries* as "property lines" that define and protect you and your emotions, values, behaviors, and attitudes. Boundaries serve two important functions. First, they *define* us. Boundaries show what we are and are not; what we agree and disagree with; what we love and hate. Boundaries also *protect* us. Boundaries keep good things in and bad things out. Then, last time we met, we

# PLANNING NOTES

_____

_____

_____

_____

_____

_____

_____

_____

_____

_____

_____

_____

*Session Three*

# Taking God on a Date

## OVERVIEW

In this session you will

- Define and compare upside-down and right-side-up dating.

- Look at several aspects of your spiritual life that you will want to bring into a relationship.

- Learn how to evaluate the fruit of a dating relationship.

- Be encouraged to develop a relationship in which each person is challenging the other to "walk the talk."

35

_____

_____

_____

_____

_____

_____

_____

_____

_____

_____

_____

_____

_____

talked about truthfulness, the best boundary of all. We looked at six kinds of deception common in the world of dating, and we saw that where there is deception, there is no relationship.

Now let's turn to page 35.

→ Today we're going to talk about how to take God on a date. We will define and compare upside-down and right-side-up dating. We will look at several aspects of your spiritual life that you will want to bring into a relationship. We will learn how to evaluate the fruit of a dating relationship. And we will be encouraged to develop a relationship in which each person is challenging the other to "walk the talk."

Before we look at the first video, let me ask you a question. Have you ever heard a famous person being asked about his or her reportedly "newfound faith"? Dr. Townsend talks about hearing a well-known musician being asked about his faith. The host commented on how glad he was that the artist was a Christian and asked the artist to tell the TV audience about how he came to the faith. The musician said, "Well, I always knew there was somebody up there." "Fantastic!" applauded the host. "What a great testimony to the saving power of Jesus!"

Dr. Townsend thought, *Could you be reading into those words what you want to hear?* He wasn't questioning the artist's faith—that's between him and God. Dr. Townsend was questioning how the host interpreted the musician's statement. It seemed that he so much wanted the musician to be a Christian that whatever he said would have been fantastic.

This sort of thinking is also common in the dating arena. You get connected to someone you are really drawn to, and you hope against hope that God is a part of his or her life and of the life of the relationship. Sometimes your hope bends the realities of the situation. To avoid this trap, consider Dr. Cloud and Dr. Townsend's comments in the following video segment "Right-Side-Up Dating."

# 32 MINUTES  DISCOVERY

## 6 minutes  *Video Segment 1: "Right-Side-Up Dating"*

Remind the participants that key points from the video segment can be found on page 36 in the Participant's Guide if they would like to review them at a later time.

View Video Segment 1: "Right-Side-Up Dating."

# PLANNING NOTES

_____

_____

_____

_____

_____

_____

_____

_____

_____

_____

_____

_____

### OVERVIEW

In this session you will

- Define and compare upside-down and right-side-up dating.

- Look at several aspects of your spiritual life that you will want to bring into a relationship.

- Learn how to evaluate the fruit of a dating relationship.

- Be encouraged to develop a relationship in which each person is challenging the other to "walk the talk."

35

---

### VIDEO SEGMENT
#### *Right-Side-Up Dating*

- The issue is not how to fit our spiritual life into our dating life; rather, it is how to fit our dating life into our spiritual life. The right-side-up approach is to bring dating before God and ask for his guidance.

- Dependence on a date for the status of one's relationship with God can be a form of idolatry.

- When we demand that dating bring us the love, fulfillment, or desire we want without allowing God to point the way, we run the risk of going to the creation rather than the Creator as our ultimate source of life.

- Surrendering all of your life to God is the first and necessary step of bringing dating in line with God.

- Does your dating relationship bring you closer to God or push you further away? To evaluate the fruit of your dating relationship, ask yourself these questions:

Does the person challenge you spiritually, rather than you having to be the impetus?


Do you experience spiritual growth from interacting with that person?


Are you drawn to the transcendent God through that person?

---

Do you have an alliance with the other person in your spiritual walks?


Is the spiritual connection based on reality? Is the person authentic as well as spiritual?


Is the relationship a place of mutual vulnerability about weaknesses and sins?

Drs. Cloud and Townsend make some good points. For instance, when we're dating, we desire God *and* we desire a person. Sometimes we don't know if those desires are working together or not. And that's just one reason why it's difficult to navigate through the spiritual dimension of dating. We may also find ourselves wondering if this is the person God has for us or if we're spiritually compatible. We may struggle to know how to bring God into the relationship; we may not know how to relate spiritually; and we may try hard to avoid disagreements about spiritual matters. We may even find ourselves in denial about conflicts. Key to issues like these is taking an appropriate stance toward dating and your spiritual life. The issue is not how to fit your spiritual life into your dating life; rather, it is how to fit your dating life into your spiritual life.

It is a great experience to begin to unveil yourself to your date spiritually. As you become safer, you can share deeper parts of yourself, thereby growing closer to each other and to God. As Dr. Townsend said, there are several aspects of your spiritual life that you will want to bring into the relationship: your faith story, values, struggles, spiritual autonomy, and friendships.

## *18 minutes*

## *Let's Talk: Bringing Your Spiritual Life into a Dating Relationship*

Participant's Guide page 38.

### Directions

1.  On pages 38–41 you'll see five aspects of your life that you will want to bring into an open and spiritually healthy dating relationship. You'll also notice that one question in each section is italicized. Those are this week's "Boundary Building" exercise for you to do at home, so leave those alone for now.
2.  We will be splitting up into five groups. I'm going to assign each group one of these five aspects of life. Your group will have 8 minutes to read through your section and discuss the questions.
3.  After I call the group back together, a spokesperson from each group will share the group's ideas with the rest of us.

Assign one of the five aspects of life to each group. Let the participants know when there is 1 minute remaining. Call the group back together after 8 minutes.

Have each spokesperson share the group's answers to the questions. If time is limited, have the spokesperson address only the issue of why it is important that this particular aspect of life be shared with one's date.

## LET'S TALK

### Bringing Your Spiritual Life into a Dating Relationship

**DIRECTIONS**

1. Below you'll see five aspects of your life that you will want to bring into an open and spiritually healthy dating relationship. You'll also notice that one question in each section is italicized. Those are this week's "Boundary Building" exercise for you to do at home, so leave those alone for now.
2. You will be splitting up into five groups. The leader will be assigning each group one of these five aspects of life. Your group will have 8 minutes to read through your section and discuss the questions.
3. After the group is called back together, a spokesperson from each group will share their group's ideas with the rest of us.

**FIVE ASPECTS OF LIFE**

1. **Faith story.** Every believer has a story of how their relationship with God began and developed.
   Why is your faith story important to share?

   What elements of someone else's faith story (a date's, a friend's, or a relative's) have encouraged you and drawn you closer to that person and to the Lord?

   *What faith story do you—or could you—share with a date?*

2. **Values.** Your values are the architecture of who you are. They are comprised of what you believe is most important in life and how you conduct your life in accordance with these beliefs.
   Why is each of the following values important to share with a date?

   - Theology
   - Finances
   - Calling in life
   - Family
   - Relationships
   - Sex
   - Job and career
   - Social issues

   *How do you or could you make each of the following values part of your dating world? What questions could you ask and what stances would you take?*

   - Theology
   - Calling in life
   - Relationships
   - Job and career
   - Finances

   - Family
   - Sex
   - Social issues

3. **Struggles.** Failure, loss, confusion, mistakes, and learning experiences are part of the life of faith. To know a person's spiritual walk is also to know the times they stumbled in the darkness.
   Why is it important to share with a date such struggles as periods of being unsure about God's care or existence; living life apart from God; spiritual adolescence (challenging everything you've been taught); or times of self-absorption when you neglected your spiritual growth?

   When, if ever, has being brought into a date's or a friend's spiritual struggle made that relationship richer, if not easier? Explain.

   *Which of your own spiritual struggles do you need to share at an appropriate time if you want to be known in a dating relationship? How would you describe or explain the issue(s)?*

4. **Spiritual autonomy.** People who are trying to pull off a successful dating relationship need to know that the other person is spiritually autonomous. That is, he has his own walk with God that he pursues on a regular basis, regardless of his circumstances.
   Why is it important to date (and marry!) someone who is owning his or her spiritual walk? For starters, consider Ecclesiastes 4:10.

   Why is time key to determining whether your date is truly spiritually autonomous?

   *Are you spiritually autonomous? If so, how would you deal with a date when it became obvious that the person and you were not spiritually autonomous? Or, if you and the person you are dating aren't spiritually autonomous, what steps will you take to get there? For instance, what spiritual discipline will you focus on? Be specific.*

5. **Friendships.** You can learn a lot about people by the sort of friends they keep. The number of Christian friends they have, for instance, can be a telling detail.
   Why is it important to know (not just know about) your date's friends?

   Think of a friend or a date. What does that person's friendships reveal?

   *What do your friendships reveal about you, your priorities, your faith, your spiritual health?*

   These questions about a person's spiritual condition are not meant to be tools for judgmental scrutiny. Instead, they are intended to help both you and your date to examine your hearts and your relationships with God and each other.

Great discussion! Dr. Cloud and Dr. Townsend have other points for us to consider about taking God into a dating relationship. Let's hear from them now.

**6 minutes**

## Video Segment 2: "Walking Your Talk"

> Remind the participants that key points from the video segment can be found on page 42 of the Participant's Guide if they would like to review them at a later time.

> View Video Segment 2: "Walking Your Talk."

**10 minutes**

## On Your Own: Spiritual Health and Growth

> Participant's Guide page 43.

Having been challenged to help our date grow spiritually, to grow spiritually ourselves, and to walk our talk as we date, let's talk now about spiritual health and growth. Please turn to page 43.

### Directions

We will be doing this as an individual exercise. Work through the questions. (You might want to spend the most time on question 4.) You will have 10 minutes to do this exercise. Any questions?

> Let the participants know when there is 1 minute remaining. Call the group back together after 10 minutes.

Please turn to page 45.

**2 minutes**

## A Few More Thoughts on . . . Spiritual Compatibility and Dating

Before you enter or reenter the world of dating, ask yourselves the following questions:

→ Which of the following are issues for you? Make them a topic of both prayer and awareness.

   • Wanting your date to be COMPATIBLE spiritually
   • Trying to CHANGE the other person spiritually

## VIDEO SEGMENT
### Walking Your Talk

- Don't interpret religious agreement or passivity on your date's part as spiritual compatibility!

- It is important to be in agreement on the fundamentals of the Christian faith, but you also want to be in relationship with someone who has thought through their own spiritual issues deeply and individually and has reached their own conclusions.

- Fall in love with someone who is passionate about matters of faith, enough to wrestle with and discuss their meaning with you. Some of the most meaningful times of growth for dates can be when two people argue, read the Bible, and come to terms on spiritual matters.

- Watch to see how your date integrates faith into real life. Religious people *know* the Truth, but spiritual people *do* it.

- Be part of each other's spiritual growth and conduct. Even if you do not end up marrying each other, take the stance that during your tenure as dates, you both will grow spiritually.

- We encourage you to develop a relationship in which you are both challenging each other to "walk your talk."

- Evidence of walking your talk is found in the ability to love and be humble. Truly spiritual people know they don't "have it all together." In fact, the opposite is true: they know how deep their failings are and how much they need God's grace. As a result, they are able to empty themselves and love other people.

## ON YOUR OWN
### Spiritual Health and Growth

We will be doing this as an individual exercise. Work through the questions. (You might want to spend the most time on question 4.) You will have 10 minutes to do this exercise.

**The design issue.** The deepest part of you is made to desire spiritual intimacy with another person. If that part of you is working properly, you will seek out healthy spirituality in others.

1. What do your relationships (past and present, dating and otherwise) show about whether you are seeking out healthy spirituality in others?

**Spiritual development path.** Spiritual development means that you are not who you were nor are you who you will be.

2. What is good advice if a person's date is still questioning the content and meaning of Christianity?

**Areas of belief and practice.** As you get to know your date spiritually, you will need to decide what disagreements about belief and practice you can live with and which you can't.

3. What is a wise course of action if your date's beliefs or spiritual practices are a red flag?

**Differences in spiritual level.** Many people struggle with questions about dating others who are at a different level than they are spiritually.

4. In light of what you've learned in this session, what advice would you give the first party mentioned in each pair listed below?

   Christian who loves a non-Christian

   Committed Christian who is dating an uncommitted Christian

   Mature Christian who is getting serious about a new Christian

## A FEW MORE THOUGHTS ON . . .
## SPIRITUAL COMPATIBILITY AND DATING

Which of the following are issues for you? Make them a topic of both prayer and awareness.

- Wanting your date to be _____ spiritually

- Trying to _____ the other person spiritually

- Denying spiritual _____ in the relationship

- Missing our own spiritual _____ and focusing on our partner's

- Being afraid to address spiritual _____

Second, what are you currently doing to _____ in Christ and _____ his paths—or what could you be doing?

> As we continue to grow in Christ, it becomes easier to love and invest our hearts wisely and well in our dating lives.

- Denying spiritual CONFLICTS in the relationship
- Missing our own spiritual WEAKNESSES and focusing on our partner's
- Being afraid to address spiritual ISSUES

Second, what are you currently doing to GROW in Christ and WALK his paths—or what could you be doing?

As we continue to grow in Christ, it becomes easier to love and invest our hearts wisely and well in our dating lives.

## 2 MINUTES    SUMMARY

Dr. Cloud and Dr. Townsend have given us many reasons why it is important to take God on a date, to have him be part of your dating relationships. Dating is not to be entered into lightly, or apart from the Lord. As I mentioned earlier, this week's "Boundary Building" exercise asks you to answer the italicized questions in "Bringing Your Spiritual Life into a Dating Relationship" so you can work on living out the lessons of this session.

Now let's close in prayer.

## 1 minute    *Closing Prayer*

Lord God, you do indeed want to be Lord of our life, every aspect of it. We want that, too, yet we struggle to live that way. Teach us to live with you as our priority even if it costs us in our dating relationships. And grow our knowledge and love for you so that we are "walking my talk" and living with integrity a life that honors you. In Jesus' name. Amen.

# PLANNING NOTES

_____

_____

_____

_____

_____

_____

_____

_____

_____

_____

_____

_____

_____

_____

_____

_____

_____

_____

_____

_____

_____

_____

_____

_____

---

Session Three: *Taking God on a Date*                          45

## A FEW MORE THOUGHTS ON ...
## SPIRITUAL COMPATIBILITY AND DATING

Which of the following are issues for you? Make them a topic of both prayer and awareness.

- Wanting your date to be _____ spiritually

- Trying to _____ the other person spiritually

- Denying spiritual _____ in the relationship

- Missing our own spiritual _____ and focusing on our partner's

- Being afraid to address spiritual _____

Second, what are you currently doing to _____ in Christ and _____ his paths—or what could you be doing?

> As we continue to grow in Christ, it becomes easier to love and invest our hearts wisely and well in our dating lives.

---

46                          *Boundaries in Dating Paticipant's Guide*

## Boundary Building

Answer the italicized questions in "Bringing Your Spiritual Life into a Dating Relationship" so you can work on living out the lessons of this session.

## Suggested Reading

For more thoughts on this session's topic, read chapter 3 in *Boundaries in Dating:* "Take God on a Date." For a more thorough self-evaluation, look at chapter 3 in the *Boundaries in Dating Workbook*.

# Session Four

# Setting Boundaries on Aloneness and on the Past

## BEFORE YOU LEAD

### Key Points

- Dr. Cloud and Dr. Townsend offer seven signs of giving up healthy boundaries because of the fear of being alone.
- To be happy in a relationship, and to pick the kind of relationship that is going to be the kind you desire, you must be able to be happy without one.
- In order to cure your fear of being alone, you need to put a boundary around your wish for a relationship. Deal with the nature of that wish and the fears involved. Cure that fear first, and then find a relationship.
- Be vulnerable in your support settings. Have a full life of spiritual growth, personal growth, vocational growth, altruistic service, hobbies, intellectual growth, and the like. And pursue wholeness: work on the issues that are in your soul.
- The first dating problem is denying that your past demonstrates a problem!
- Understanding the past helps us grow. So does developing a healthy fear of not dealing with your past dating patterns.
- Be afraid of repeating your past.

### Synopsis

Some people just can't stand being alone, and their fear of being alone keeps them from having boundaries with bad relationships. Simply put, they would rather have a bad dating relationship than no dating relationship at all. Dr. Cloud and Dr. Townsend offer seven signs of giving up healthy boundaries because of the fear of being alone:

1. Putting up with behavior that is disrespectful
2. Giving in to things that are not in accord with your values
3. Settling for less than you know you really desire or need

4. Staying in a relationship that you know has passed its deadline
5. Going back into a relationship that you know should be over
6. Getting into a relationship that you know is not going anywhere
7. Smothering the person you are dating with excessive needs or control

Surely there are other signs of the fear of being alone. But the point is, in cases like these, a person's dating is ruled by their internal isolation, rather than by their God, goals, values, and spiritual commitments. Their fear of aloneness makes them get involved in relationships that they know are not going to last. It also keeps them from being alone long enough to grow into people who do not have to be in a relationship in order to be happy. There is a very important rule in dating and romance: To be happy in a relationship, and to pick the kind of relationship that is going to be the kind you desire, you must be able to be happy without one. A good dating boundary in regards to aloneness would be: In order to cure your fear of being alone, put a boundary around your wish for a dating relationship. Deal with the nature of that wish and the fears involved. Cure that fear first, and then find a relationship.

A second important boundary is a boundary with your past. In research for the book *Boundaries in Dating,* married people indicated that they wished they could have benefited more from their dating experiences. Evaluate your dating past. Did you date too seriously? Was it difficult for you to be honest? Did you neglect friendships? Did your life revolve around dating instead of your dating being part of a balanced life? When you recognize patterns like these, you can begin to work through them.

It's important to set a boundary with your past, that is, to deal with your old dating patterns as something you are not destined to continue. Your past can be your best friend or worst enemy in terms of helping you develop the right sort of dating relationships. The past is the repository of all your trial-and-error experiences. It can provide a great deal of necessary information on what to do and what to avoid in dating, either through the satisfaction of doing it right or the pain of doing it wrong. To blithely skip over the past is to ignore important aspects of reality, while to pay attention to what you have done before is to take ownership of your present and future. Also, realize that the first dating problem is denying that your past demonstrates a problem!

So if you tend to get with your buddies or girlfriends and have gripe sessions about the lack of quality dating material in the world, do something constructive for a change. Ask them, God, and yourself the same question: What can I learn from my dating past that will help me avoid bad things or experience good things in the future? This requires more work than griping and is nowhere near as enjoyable, but it does tend to produce good results. An even more pointed question is "What have I done to contribute to my dating problems today?" This is not about self-condemnation. Instead, it is about quest for truth and reality to free you up from repeating past mistakes. It's about setting and maintaining a healthy and helpful boundary with your past.

## Recommended Reading

"Dating Won't Cure a Lonely Heart" and "Don't Repeat the Past," chapters 4 and 5 of *Boundaries in Dating*

# Session Four

## Setting Boundaries on Aloneness and on the Past

| **3 MINUTES** | **INTRODUCTION** |
|---|---|

### 1 minute — Welcome

> Call the group together and welcome the participants to Session 4, "Setting Boundaries on Aloneness and on the Past."

### 1 minute — *Opening Prayer*

Thank you, God, that you want to be involved in every part of our lives. As we saw last time, you want very much to be an important part of our dating. Be with us now as we learn more about dating in a way that honors you and is healthy for us. We pray in Jesus' name. Amen.

### 1 minute — *Review and Overview*

> Participant's Guide page 47.

Taking God on a date, including him in our dating lives, may have been either a new idea or an important reminder to you. As we just prayed, God does want to be involved in every part of our lives. So it was good for each of us to consider whether we are in fact consulting him about our dating, following the guidelines he sets forth in Scripture as we date, and encouraging our dates to grow in Christ even as they encourage our spiritual growth.

Let's turn to page 47.

➜ Today we're going to look at our dating patterns to see if we're expecting dating to do something it isn't designed to do or if

# PLANNING NOTES

_____

_____

_____

_____

_____

_____

_____

_____

_____

_____

_____

_____

_____

*Session Four*

## Setting Boundaries on Aloneness and on the Past

### OVERVIEW

In this session you will

- Review seven signs of giving up healthy boundaries because of the fear of being alone.
- Learn why it is important to put a boundary around your wish for relationship—and how to do that.
- See what your past dating patterns show you about yourself.

47

_____

_____

_____

_____

_____

_____

_____

_____

_____

_____

_____

_____

_____

we're repeating past mistakes in our dating patterns. Since dating won't cure a lonely heart, we will first learn why it's important to set boundaries on our wish for a relationship—and how to do that. We'll also see what our past dating patterns show us about ourselves and realize that we are not destined to continue any unhealthy patterns we discover.

## 47 MINUTES DISCOVERY

**6 minutes**

### Video Segment 1: "A Boundary around Your Wish for Relationship"

Let's hear what Dr. Townsend and Dr. Cloud have to say about setting boundaries on aloneness.

> Remind the participants that key points from the video segment can be found on page 48 of the Participant's Guide if they would like to review them at a later time.

> View Video Segment 1: "A Boundary around Your Wish for Relationship."

In order to cure your fear of being alone, put a boundary around your wish for a dating relationship. There is nothing wrong with the desire for a relationship; just don't let it be a demand that controls you. Deal with the nature of that wish and the fears involved. Cure that fear first, and then find a relationship. How do you cure that fear? The following exercise offers some pointers.

**10 minutes**

### On Your Own: Curing the Fear of Being Alone

> Participant's Guide page 49.

### Directions

Turn to pages 49–51 and take 10 minutes to consider the questions you find there.

> Let the participants know when there is 1 minute remaining. Call the group back together after 10 minutes.

You've been considering an important boundary in dating: the boundary around your wish for a relationship against the fear of being alone. Now we're going to consider a second important boundary, a boundary with your past. Dr. Cloud and Dr. Townsend will explain.

## VIDEO SEGMENT

### *A Boundary around Your Wish for Relationship*

- Some people just can't stand being alone, and their fear of being alone keeps them from having boundaries with bad relationships.

- Dr. Cloud and Dr. Townsend offer these seven signs of giving up healthy boundaries because of the fear of being alone:

  1. Putting up with behavior that is disrespectful
  2. Giving in to things that are not in accord with your values
  3. Settling for less than you know you really desire or need
  4. Staying in a relationship that you know has passed its deadline
  5. Going back into a relationship that you know should be over
  6. Getting into a relationship that you know is not going anywhere
  7. Smothering the person you are dating with excessive needs or control

In cases like these, a peron's dating is ruled by their internal isolation, rather than by their God, goals, values, and spiritual commitments.

- To be happy in a relationship, and to pick the kind of relationship that is going to be the kind you desire, you must be able to be happy without one.

- In order to cure your fear of being alone, put a boundary around your wish for a relationship.

## ON YOUR OWN

### *Curing the Fear of Being Alone*

**DIRECTIONS**

Take 10 minutes to consider the points you find below.

In order to cure your fear of being alone, you need to put a boundary around your wish for a dating relationship. There is nothing wrong with the desire; just don't let it be a demand that controls you. Instead, deal with the nature of that wish and the fears involved. Cure that fear first, and then find a relationship. How do you cure that fear?

1. Strengthen your relationship with God. How will you do that? Make a list of some specific action steps you can take. Then circle the step you will take this week.


2. Strengthen your relationships with safe, healthy Christians. Who in your life falls into that category—or where will you find safe, healthy Christians?


3. Get a support system to ground you so that you can make dating choices out of strength, not out of weakness or dependency.

   - Describe your support system—or jot down some ideas about developing a stronger one.

- In those supportive relationships, are you allowing yourself to be appropriately dependent, have needs, and express pain and hurts? Support your answer with specific examples of your vulnerability.


4. A person living a full life of spiritual growth, personal growth, vocational growth, altruistic service, hobbies, and intellectual growth does not have the time or inclination to be dependent on a date. We've already addressed your spiritual life. What are you doing to be active and grow in these other areas?

Personal development


Job/career


Service to others


Hobbies and recreation


Intellectual pursuits

5. In addition to having an active life, work on the issues in your soul. What issues (past childhood hurts, recurring themes and patterns in your relationships and work life, other areas of brokenness, pain, and dysfunction) are you or could you be addressing? Is a fear of aloneness related to any of these soul issues?


The best boundary against giving in to bad relationships, less-than-satisfactory relationships, or bad dynamics in a good relationship is your not being dependent on that relationship. And that is going to come from being grounded in God, grounded in a support system, working out your issues, having a full life, and pursuing wholeness. If you are doing those things, you will be less subject to saying yes when you should be saying no.

**6 minutes**

# Video Segment 2: "A Boundary with Your Past"

> Remind the participants that key points from the video segment can be found on page 52 of the Participant's Guide if they would like to review them at a later time.

> View Video Segment 2: "A Boundary with Your Past."

As you heard what Drs. Cloud and Townsend said, you may have thought about your own problematic patterns of dating. Maybe you tend to go too quickly, to adapt to your date's desires, or to allow the relationship to rule you. Patterns like these hinder progress toward depth, commitment, and marriage.

A good element of setting boundaries with your dating past is a healthy fear of the consequences of repeating the past. This fear is a healthy concern over our accountability to God for how we conduct our lives. So—be afraid, be very afraid—of the right things. Let's talk now about some of these "right things."

Please turn to page 53.

**10 minutes**

# A Few More Thoughts on . . . a Healthy Fear of the Past

> Participant's Guide page 53.

➜ First, be afraid of RUINING your present relationship. Don't neglect your past just because your present is good. Doing the hard work of growth now can help prevent problems in the future. Why is a good dating relationship an opportune time to do some hard work of growth?

> Solicit answers from the group. Possible answers may include: "We can practice healthier behaviors"; "We can practice being honest and open"; "We can learn to apologize when we offend the person we're dating"; and perhaps even "We can ask someone to hold us accountable in areas where we want to grow."

➜ Second, be afraid of STAYING with your present relationship. If a person is in a relationship that isn't so good, how might looking at his or her past help?

> Solicit answers from the group. Possible answers may include: "We can see that staying doesn't make the eventual leaving any easier" or "We'll see that our unhealthy ways get unhealthier."

# PLANNING NOTES

_____

_____

_____

_____

_____

_____

_____

_____

_____

_____

_____

_____

_____

_____

_____

_____

_____

_____

_____

_____

_____

---

52                    *Boundaries in Dating Paticipant's Guide*

### VIDEO SEGMENT
#### *A Boundary with Your Past*

- Begin to evaluate your dating past. Did you date too seriously? Was it difficult for you to be honest? Did you neglect friendships? Did your life revolve around dating instead of your dating being part of a balanced life? When you recognize patterns like these, you can begin to work through them.

- Your past can provide a great deal of necessary information on what to do and what to avoid in dating, either through the satisfaction of doing it right, or the pain of doing it wrong.

- To blithely skip over the past is to ignore important aspects of reality, while to pay attention to what you have done before is to take ownership of your present and future.

- The first dating problem is denying that your past demonstrates a problem!

- Understanding our past helps us grow.

- Be afraid of your past: have a healthy fear of the consequences of repeating the past.

- Ask your buddies or girlfriends, God, and yourself the same question: What can I learn from my dating past that will help me avoid bad things or experience good things in the future?

---

Session Four: *Setting Boundaries on Aloneness and the Past*      53

### A FEW MORE THOUGHTS ON . . .
### A HEALTHY FEAR OF THE PAST

- Be afraid of _____ your present relationship. Don't neglect your past just because your present is good. Doing the hard work of growth now can help prevent problems in the future.

- Be afraid of _____ with your present relationship.

- Be afraid of being _____. Perhaps in the past you have invested in and trusted someone who was not very trustworthy. Look at that past: Consider why you have been hurt along the way.

- Be afraid of _____.

- Be afraid of reducing your _____. People who haven't learned lessons from the past are less free to be themselves, grow, and make decisions.

- We need to clearly understand both the prospects we face if things remain the same as well as the risks of not learning and growing from our past. This two-fold understanding helps us bear the pain of changing.

➜ Third, be afraid of being INJURED. Perhaps in the past you have invested in and trusted someone who was not very trustworthy. Look at that past: Consider why you have been hurt along the way. What can a person do—what can you do—to avoid these same kinds of hurts? What tools could help prevent that hurt in the future?

> Solicit answers from the group. Possible answers may include: "Have your friends get to know your date so they can confirm your sense of whether he or she is trustworthy" or "Sometimes you need to ask questions when someone says something you're not quite sure you should believe."

➜ Fourth, be afraid of WASTING TIME. You probably have a mental time frame for marriage. Why is it wise to be afraid of wasting time? And why does working on the past keep us from wasting time?

> Solicit answers from the group. Possible answers may include: "We can see that waiting for someone to change into marriageable material is futile" or "Looking at the past can help us want to be very careful and very wise with the time we have."

➜ Fifth, be afraid of reducing your PROSPECTS. People who haven't learned lessons from the past are less free to be themselves, grow, and make decisions. For example, a woman may be drawn to inconsistent, ambivalent men who can't commit. She may not, then, be excited by a stable, available, and accessible man. Her past may label such a man as boring and stodgy. Recognizing past dating problems enables you to open yourself to future healthy dating prospects. Why does failing to learn from the past mean less freedom to be yourself? And why does this lack of freedom mean fewer prospects for healthy and potentially rewarding relationships?

> Solicit answers from the group. Possible answers may include: "If we don't see our mistakes in the past, we may not be aware of what we're doing. Then we'll act out of habit—and that's not being ourselves" or "It's good to figure out what it is about the people we've dated that hasn't made them a great fit with us. Then we'll be able to look around and see other kinds of people as potentially better matches."

We need to clearly understand both the prospects we face if things remain the same as well as the risks of not learning and growing from our

# PLANNING NOTES

_____

_____

_____

_____

_____

_____

_____

_____

_____

_____

_____

_____

_____

---

## A FEW MORE THOUGHTS ON ...
## A HEALTHY FEAR OF THE PAST

- Be afraid of _____ your present relationship. Don't neglect your past just because your present is good. Doing the hard work of growth now can help prevent problems in the future.

- Be afraid of _____ with your present relationship.

- Be afraid of being _____. Perhaps in the past you have invested in and trusted someone who was not very trustworthy. Look at that past: Consider why you have been hurt along the way.

- Be afraid of _____.

- Be afraid of reducing your _____. People who haven't learned lessons from the past are less free to be themselves, grow, and make decisions.

- We need to clearly understand both the prospects we face if things remain the same as well as the risks of not learning and growing from our past. This two-fold understanding helps us bear the pain of changing.

---

_____

_____

_____

_____

_____

_____

_____

_____

_____

_____

_____

_____

_____

past. This two-fold understanding helps us bear the pain of changing.

> → Thanks for sharing. As it says in your Participant's Guides, we need to clearly understand both the prospects we face if things remain the same, as well as the risks of not learning and growing from our past. This twofold understanding helps us bear the pain of changing.

**15 minutes**

## *Let's Talk: Why the Past Still Rules*

> Participant's Guide page 54.

So, you may be thinking, *If there are so many good reasons to work through our past dating patterns, why do people have difficulty doing so?* There are several reasons. Please turn now to page 54.

## Directions

1. I will be dividing you into four groups and assigning each group one of the four deterrents to working through and overcoming past dating patterns.
2. Read through and discuss the questions assigned to your group, making sure that each person gets a chance to share.
3. Choose a representative to share your group's ideas with the large group after the exercise is over.
4. You will have 5 minutes to answer your group's questions. Any questions?

> Let the participants know when there is 1 minute remaining. Call the group back together after 5 minutes.

The first group talked about lack of maturity. What evidence in a person's life would suggest that she is more interested in living only in the present than in learning from the past and growing for the future?

> Solicit answers from the group. Possible answers include: reluctance to talk about past relationships; an attitude that suggests she is never the guilty party when a relationship ends; failure to be involved in any kind of Bible study or other avenue of personal growth.

The first group also discussed what safe individuals can do to help someone grow in love and truth. Who would like to comment on that?

> Solicit answers from the group. Possible answers include: encouraging a person to talk about the past; lovingly speaking the truth they see about their friend's past dating patterns; or inviting that someone to join in whatever they are doing to grow for the future.

## A FEW MORE THOUGHTS ON . . .
## A HEALTHY FEAR OF THE PAST

- Be afraid of _____ your present relationship. Don't neglect your past just because your present is good. Doing the hard work of growth now can help prevent problems in the future.

- Be afraid of _____ with your present relationship.

- Be afraid of being _____. Perhaps in the past you have invested in and trusted someone who was not very trustworthy. Look at that past: Consider why you have been hurt along the way.

- Be afraid of _____.

- Be afraid of reducing your _____. People who haven't learned lessons from the past are less free to be themselves, grow, and make decisions.

- We need to clearly understand both the prospects we face if things remain the same as well as the risks of not learning and growing from our past. This two-fold understanding helps us bear the pain of changing.

## LET'S TALK
### *Why the Past Still Rules*

**DIRECTIONS**

1. The leader will be dividing you into four groups and assigning each group one of the four deterrents to working through and overcoming past dating patterns.
2. Read through and discuss the questions assigned to your group, making sure that each person gets a chance to share.
3. Choose a representative to share your group's ideas with the large group after the exercise is over.
4. You will have 5 minutes to answer your group's questions.

*Lack of maturity.* One indicator of character maturity is the ability to be aware, curious, and concerned about one's past patterns.

1. What evidence in a person's life would suggest that she is more interested in living only in the present than in learning from the past and growing for the future?

2. What can safe individuals do to help someone grow in love and truth?

*Fear of the unknown.* Fearing the unknown—worrying about what might happen if you change—can stall the growth process.

1. Which do many, if not most, people prefer: a known bad thing or an unknown thing? Why?

2. When being honest in a dating relationship is an unknown thing for a person, what can close friends do to help so that the unknown of honesty can become a known good thing?

*Fear of the known.* Some people repeat the past because they have tried to change their patterns and suffered greatly for some reason. The pain was sufficient to stop their attempt to change.

1. When can attempts to change and grow result in pain?

2. As the old Alcoholics Anonymous saying goes, change occurs when the pain of remaining the same is greater than the pain of changing. What pain, if any, are you living with in a current relationship? What pain of changing seems worse than that pain?

*Isolation.* One major obstacle to resolving the past is the state of being cut off from the source of life, which is relationship with God and others. Relationship is the fuel which makes change and growth possible.

1. When, if ever, have you experienced the comfort, support, or reality of relationship? Be specific. How did you benefit?

2. If a person doesn't have enough support to deal with the past and resolve it, to make change and growth possible, where can he or she go for fuel?

The second group discussed fear of the unknown. Which do many people prefer: a known thing or an unknown thing—and why?

> Solicit answers from the group. Possible answers include: most people prefer a known thing because it's familiar, they feel they can handle it, and they don't have to change.

How can close friends help honesty become a known good thing for someone?

> Solicit answers from the group. Possible answers include: asking probing questions when a statement seems less than honest, or talking about experiences when honesty clearly paid off.

The third group looked at fear of the known, fear that has grown up around the pain that came with one time trying to change. When can attempts to change and grow result in pain?

> Solicit answers from the group. Possible answers include: when the timing is wrong; when the person doesn't have any support; when the person you are practicing with isn't trustworthy.

The fourth group talked about isolation. How have people in that group benefited from the comfort, support, or reality of relationship?

> Solicit answers from the group. Possible answers include: having others confirm their theories about their past dating patterns; encouraging them to change; giving them a safe place to try out new behaviors.

Where can people who are cut off from God and other people find relationship and, with it, the fuel that makes change and growth possible?

> Solicit answers from the group. Possible answers include church, athletic teams, bike clubs, and this class!

## 2 MINUTES    SUMMARY

It is important to understand that you must *have* a past to resolve your past. In other words, you need to be aware that your past dating patterns have been a problem and that today you want to change that pattern. Many people are totally unaware that they struggle with their past, so they end up repeating the past so much that it is inseparable from the present. In that sense, there is no past, only a continuous,

# PLANNING NOTES

_____

_____

_____

_____

_____

_____

_____

_____

_____

_____

_____

_____

---

## LET'S TALK
### *Why the Past Still Rules*

**DIRECTIONS**

1. The leader will be dividing you into four groups and assigning each group one of the four deterrents to working through and overcoming past dating patterns.
2. Read through and discuss the questions assigned to your group, making sure that each person gets a chance to share.
3. Choose a representative to share your group's ideas with the large group after the exercise is over.
4. You will have 5 minutes to answer your group's questions.

   ***Lack of maturity.*** One indicator of character maturity is the ability to be aware, curious, and concerned about one's past patterns.

1. What evidence in a person's life would suggest that she is more interested in living only in the present than in learning from the past and growing for the future?

2. What can safe individuals do to help someone grow in love and truth?

   ***Fear of the unknown.*** Fearing the unknown—worrying about what might happen if you change—can stall the growth process.

---

1. Which do many, if not most, people prefer: a known bad thing or an unknown thing? Why?

2. When being honest in a dating relationship is an unknown thing for a person, what can close friends do to help so that the unknown of honesty can become a known good thing?

   ***Fear of the known.*** Some people repeat the past because they have tried to change their patterns and suffered greatly for some reason. The pain was sufficient to stop their attempt to change.

1. When can attempts to change and grow result in pain?

2. As the old Alcoholics Anonymous saying goes, change occurs when the pain of remaining the same is greater than the pain of changing. What pain, if any, are you living with in a current relationship? What pain of changing seems worse than that pain?

   ***Isolation.*** One major obstacle to resolving the past is the state of being cut off from the source of life, which is relationship with God and others. Relationship is the fuel which makes change and growth possible.

---

1. When, if ever, have you experienced the comfort, support, or reality of relationship? Be specific. How did you benefit?

2. If a person doesn't have enough support to deal with the past and resolve it, to make change and growth possible, where can he or she go for fuel?

painful present that doesn't work for them. If this is you, ask God to help you begin to turn away from your pattern. That turning away—that repentance—creates a break between past and present, so that you can then heal from the effects of the past.

This week, focus on the two boundaries we've been talking about. You might want to spend more time identifying any problematic patterns of your past dating. As your "Boundary Building" exercise, continue to work on "Why the Past Still Rules." Focus on the three deterrents to learning from past dating that your small group did not cover. Be sure to ask the questions of yourself as if you're the someone being referred to. That way you can learn from your past so that you won't repeat it. Also, take some time to consider whether you are hoping that relationships will numb the ache that comes with being alone. Let's close in prayer.

## *1 minute*          *Closing Prayer*

Eternal God, you are the same yesterday, today, and tomorrow. You are God of the past, the present, the future. So we ask you to help us see our dating patterns of the past, own those patterns and resolve them in the present, and grow beyond them for the future. We also need help in dealing with the aloneness some of us feel in being single. Please also show us what good things to fill our life with and where we can go to grow spiritually, personally, and intellectually in our work, our hobbies, and our service to others. Most of all, we ask you to help us live out the truth that we need you more than we need any other relationship. We look to you—and to the safe relationships that you'll provide—to change us and make us healthier and spiritually stronger. In Jesus' name. Amen.

# PLANNING NOTES

_____

_____

_____

_____

_____

_____

_____

_____

_____

_____

_____

_____

_____

## Boundary Building

During the week, work some more on the exercise "Why the Past Still Rules." Focus on the three deterrents to learning from past dating that your small group did not cover. Be sure to ask the questions of yourself as if you're the someone being referred to. That way you can learn from your past so that you don't repeat it. Also take some time to consider whether you are hoping that relationships will numb the ache that comes with being alone.

## Suggested Reading

For more thoughts on this session's topic, read chapters 4 and 5 in *Boundaries in Dating:* "Dating Won't Cure a Lonely Heart" and "Don't Repeat the Past." For a more thorough self-evaluation, look at chapters 4 and 5 in the *Boundaries in Dating Workbook*.

# Session Five

# Whom Should I Be Dating? Part 1

## BEFORE YOU LEAD

### Key Points

- Consider the character of the person you want to date. Look at your "boundaries of choices," your requirements regarding the people you date. There are basically four areas that require examination:
  1. Are your preferences too limiting? Do you need to be more open?
  2. Are some preferences more important than you realize? Value them!
  3. Which imperfections in a person's character are minor? You'll need to learn to deal with them.
  4. Which imperfections in a person's character are major? These are totally off-limits. You should never have to live with them.

- Because of the very nature of human beings, you are always going to be dating someone with flaws, and relationships will be imperfect. But there are flaws you can live with, and those you can't. Serious character flaws can injure and destroy you.

- Protect yourself by knowing what you feel and value, and have the courage to stick to what you value for your dating life. Ultimately you will get what you value. Value good things, and say no to things that destroy.

- Another question related to "Whom should I be dating?" is "What should I do when opposites attract?" You should use and appreciate the abilities of those who have what you don't. However, the danger occurs when you make opposing styles or abilities a basis for relationship.

- Opposite-driven relationships often confuse dependency with true love. Dependency is only part of love.

- In mature couples, opposite traits are simply not a major issue. The two people are not drawn to opposite traits due to their own deficits; they are drawn to the values they share, such as love, responsibility, forgiveness, honesty, and spirituality. Attraction based on values is much more mature than attraction based on what you don't have inside.

- Make oppositeness a nonissue. Look more for character, love, and values than "who has what." Don't fall for an introvert simply because you are an extrovert. Fall for someone who calls you into love, growth, and God. And then appreciate the unique differences each can bring to the relationship.

## *Synopsis*

As Dr. Cloud told one young woman, "You are initially attracted to a person's outsides, but after awhile you'll experience his insides. His character is what you will experience long-term and be in relationship with over time." So, as you consider the character of the person you want to date, look at your "boundaries of choices"—at your requirements for the people you date. If you know ahead of time what you will not put up with in a dating relationship, you could save yourself from a season or even a lifetime of misery. On the other hand, you might be too rigid in your preferences and closing yourself off to some good options.

There are basically four areas that require examination:

1. Are your preferences too limiting? Do you need to be more open?
2. Are some preferences more important than you realize? Value them!
3. Which imperfections in a person's character are minor? You'll need to learn to deal with them.
4. Which imperfections in a person's character are major? These are totally off-limits. You should never have to live with them.

If you are dealing with a person who injures you, leaves you feeling bad about yourself and love, and hurts you in other ways, you are dealing with things you should not be allowing. The best test is always your experience of the person. Protect yourself by knowing what you feel and value, and have the courage to stick to what you value for your dating life. Ultimately you will get what you value. Value good things, and say no to things that destroy.

A question related to "Whom should I be dating?" is "What should I do when opposites attract?" The idea of complementary gifts and strengths is good for us emotionally, in more than one way. We have to learn humility to ask people for what we don't possess, and that helps us grow. For example, if your date is perceptive in relationships, you might ask him why you are struggling in your relationship with your roommate. We also can grow from the competencies of others; however, the danger occurs when we make opposing styles or abilities a *basis* for relationship.

Opposite-driven relationships often confuse dependency with true love. That is, people may feel intense longings and attractions for an "opposite" person. They may appreciate the "completion" they feel with that person. But they run the risk of simply needing that person for those functions and of never giving the true loving feelings any relationship needs to grow and flourish. Dependency is only part of love; it is not the full expression of love. The full expression of love is to give back from a full heart.

Dr. Cloud and Dr. Townsend have seen that the degree of attraction opposites have for each other is often diagnostic of the couple's maturity. In mature couples, opposite traits are simply not a major issue. The two people are not drawn to opposite traits due to their own deficits; they are drawn to the values they share, such as love, responsibility, forgiveness, honesty, and spirituality. Attraction based on values is much more mature than attraction based on what you don't have inside.

Make oppositeness a nonissue. Look more for character, love, and values than which one of you has what qualities. Don't fall for an introvert simply because you are an extrovert. Fall for someone who calls you into love, growth, and God. And then appreciate the unique differences you each bring to the relationship.

## Recommended Reading

"What You Can Live With and What You Can't Live With" and "Beware When Opposites Attract," chapters 6 and 9 of *Boundaries in Dating*

# Session Five
# Whom Should I Be Dating? Part 1

## 3 MINUTES    INTRODUCTION

### 1 minute    Welcome

> Call the group together and welcome the participants to Session 5, "Whom Should I Be Dating? Part 1."

### 1 minute    Opening Prayer

Thank you, Lord, for the groundwork we've laid in these past four sessions. Now we're getting to what may be the key issue for many of us—whom should we date? May we be open to the ideas and truths presented here. May we be made aware of how you would have us change and of how you may be directing our paths by our discussions here today. In Jesus' name. Amen.

### 1 minute    Review and Overview

> Participant's Guide page 59.

We've defined the term *boundary,* we've talked about the importance of letting truth be an essential boundary in dating relationships, and we've looked at what it means to take God on a date, to have him be part of a dating relationship. Last time we saw that dating won't cure a lonely heart, and we realized how we can benefit—and save ourselves some heartache—by learning from our dating past. All these topics touch on the *how* of dating. In this session and the next we're going address the *who* of dating: whom should we be dating?

Let's turn to page 59.

# PLANNING NOTES

_____

_____

_____

_____

_____

_____

_____

_____

_____

_____

_____

_____

*Session Five*

# Whom Should I Be Dating? Part 1

## OVERVIEW

In this session you will

- Look at both your preferences and your requirements for the people you date.

- Consider whether those preferences and requirements are too limiting or not limiting enough.

- Learn some reasons why opposites attract—and why those connections can be unhealthy.

59

_____

_____

_____

_____

_____

_____

_____

_____

_____

_____

_____

_____

_____

_____

➜ We will look at both your preferences and your requirements for the people you date. We will consider whether those preferences and requirements are too limiting or not limiting enough. And we'll learn some reasons why opposites attract—and why those connections can be unhealthy.

As our session begins, let's hear what Dr. Cloud and Dr. Townsend have to say about what we can—and can't—live with.

## 50 MINUTES DISCOVERY

**6 minutes**

### *Video Segment 1: "What You Can—and Can't—Live With"*

> Remind the participants that key points from the video segment can be found on page 60 of the Participant's Guide if they would like to review them at a later time.

> View Video Segment 1: "What You Can — and Can't — Live With."

Dr. Cloud and Dr. Townsend make some good points, including the encouragement to be open to casually dating anyone of good character. Dating can be a time of getting to know many types of people—but not if we let our preferences get in the way and narrow the field for ourselves.

Let's talk a bit more about preferences now. Please turn to page 61 and fill in the blanks as we go along.

**10 minutes**

### *A Few More Thoughts on . . . Preferences*

> Participant's Guide page 61.

When discussing preferences, it is important to know your tastes and what is important to you, but also to stay open and flexible in dating, for you never know what might happen. At the same time, realize that you can't always trust preferences. They can stem from unhealthy causes and move us into unhealthy relationships.

### Unhealthy Preferences

➜
- Fears of INTIMACY can attract you to detached people.
- Fears of autonomy can attract you to CONTROLLING people.
- Fears of being real can attract you to PERFECTIONISTIC people.
- Fears of your own SINFULNESS can attract you to "bad" people.

# PLANNING NOTES

_____

_____

_____

_____

_____

_____

_____

_____

_____

_____

_____

_____

_____

_____

_____

_____

_____

_____

_____

_____

_____

_____

---

60                          *Boundaries in Dating Paticipant's Guide*

## VIDEO SEGMENT
### *What You Can—and Can't—Live With*

- What do you look for in a person to date seriously or marry? You could probably list a few things without any hesitation.

- Some traits (being athletic, intellectual, or witty, for instance) are differences in taste.

- Other traits have nothing to do with tastes and natural differences. These traits have to do with *character*. You are initially attracted to a person's outsides, but over time you'll experience their insides as well.

- Look at your "boundaries of choices"—your requirements for the people you date. Ask yourself:

  Are your preferences too limiting? Do you need to be more open?

  Are some preferences more important than you realize? Value them!

  Which imperfections in a person's character are minor? You'll need to learn to deal with them.

  Which imperfections in a person's character are major? These are totally off-limits. You should never have to live with them.

- You are always going to be dating someone with flaws. But, remember, there are flaws you can live with, and those you can't.

- Be open to casually dating anyone of good character. If the person is of good character, go out and have a good time.

---

Session Five: *Whom Should I Be Dating?* Part 1            61

## A FEW MORE THOUGHTS ON . . .
## PREFERENCES
### *Unhealthy Preferences*

- Fears of _____ can attract you to detached people.

- Fears of autonomy can attract you to _____ people.

- Fears of being real can attract you to _____ people.

- Fears of your own _____ can attract you to "bad" people.

- Fears of your own _____ can attract you to weak, passive people.

- Unresolved family of origin issues can attract you to someone who is like a _____ you had trouble with.

### *Good Preferences*

- *Common interests* help you determine how you spend your _____.

- *Common goals* determine how you spend your _____.

- *Common values* determine what _____ _____ you look for in a person.

- Fears of your own NEEDINESS can attract you to weak, passive people.
- Unresolved family of origin issues can attract you to someone who is like a PARENT you had trouble with.

The warning here is to observe your preferences and value them, but to be open to the fact that they may not always be good for you. God may know something about what you need and would enjoy that you don't know. So be open to casually dating anyone of good character. Get to know people who might not fit your preferences in areas like physical shape or personality type. You might have a good time and learn something about yourself as well!

## Good Preferences

Even if you decide to follow this advice and stay open to getting to know a variety of people, you'll still have your preferences. And some preferences are good to have. You will do better to date someone who shares common interests, common goals, and common values.

→ *Common interests* help you determine how you spend your FREE TIME. Most strong relationships include at least some common interests.

Why would sharing some of your interests be good for a dating relationship and someday a marriage?

> Solicit answers from the group. Possible answers may include: "Shared interests give you the chance to spend time together"; "Liking the same things means having fun together"; or "Common interests mean some common priorities."

Okay, let's move on to common goals.

→ *Common goals* determine how you spend your LIFE. Your goals will affect where you live, what career you choose, how you spend your time and money, and even how you develop your character and walk with God.

Why is it wise to know what your goals are before getting seriously involved with someone?

> Solicit answers from the group. Possible answers may include: "Goals suggest priorities" or " Goals reveal some things about a person's temperament. Is she a hard-charger? Is he a mover and a shaker?"

The third area in which preferences are important is the area of character.

# PLANNING NOTES

_____

_____

_____

_____

_____

_____

_____

_____

_____

_____

_____

_____

---

Session Five: *Whom Should I Be Dating? Part 1*          61

### A FEW MORE THOUGHTS ON . . . PREFERENCES

#### Unhealthy Preferences

- Fears of _____ can attract you to detached people.

- Fears of autonomy can attract you to _____ people.

- Fears of being real can attract you to _____ people.

- Fears of your own _____ can attract you to "bad" people.

- Fears of your own _____ can attract you to weak, passive people.

- Unresolved family of origin issues can attract you to someone who is like a _____ you had trouble with.

#### Good Preferences

- *Common interests* help you determine how you spend your _____.

- *Common goals* determine how you spend your _____.

- *Common values* determine what _____ _____ you look for in a person.

---

_____

_____

_____

_____

_____

_____

_____

_____

_____

_____

_____

_____

➜ *Common values* determine what CHARACTER TRAITS you look for in a person. You are going to experience someone's character if you stay in a relationship very long, so it's important that their character traits reflect the values that are important to you.

What traits do you value in a person's character?

> Solicit answers from the group. Possible answers may include: being moral, spiritual, responsible, competent, able to connect, and able to deal with reality.

When, if ever, have you seen someone compromise their standards regarding a person's character? Why do you think they did that?

> Solicit answers from the group. Possible answers may include: wanting to be loved/not wanting to be alone; being unable to stand strong under pressure; listening to one's heart instead of one's head; not being prayerful about a dating relationship; and not having friends to speak in love the truth they saw about character weaknesses.

Common interests, common goals, and common values—these are important preferences to consider when you choose whether or not to date a person. But remember, even if the preferences line up, you'll still have to deal with your date's minor imperfections. Please turn to page 62.

## *8 minutes*

## *On Your Own: Minor Imperfections*

> Participant's Guide page 62.

### Directions

On your own, spend some time working through the information and questions on pages 62–64. You'll have 8 minutes to complete the exercise. Any questions?

> Let the participants know when there is 1 minute remaining. Call the group back together after 8 minutes.

God can use minor imperfections to teach us how to put up with humanity, how not to be too judgmental or perfectionistic in our demands. Since you have to date sinners, decide which sins you can live with, or at least work with.

## A FEW MORE THOUGHTS ON . . . PREFERENCES
### Unhealthy Preferences

- Fears of _____ can attract you to detached people.

- Fears of autonomy can attract you to _____ people.

- Fears of being real can attract you to _____ people.

- Fears of your own _____ can attract you to "bad" people.

- Fears of your own _____ can attract you to weak, passive people.

- Unresolved family of origin issues can attract you to someone who is like a _____ you had trouble with.

### Good Preferences

- *Common interests* help you determine how you spend your _____.

- *Common goals* determine how you spend your _____.

- *Common values* determine what _____ _____ you look for in a person.

---

## ON YOUR OWN
### Minor Imperfections

**DIRECTIONS**

On your own, read through and answer the questions found below. You will have 8 minutes to complete this exercise.

No one is perfect. Every person you date will be a person who will sin and let you down. However, as you evaluate the people you date, remember a few things.

1. You can live with sinners who have the ability to see when they have wronged you, to confess it, to care about how they have hurt you, and to work hard not to continue in that pattern. Which of these four areas do you need to work on so you can be a sinner people can live with?

2. The following traits suggest that a person is able to work on their imperfections:

   A relationship with God

   Ability to see where one is wrong

   Ability to be honest

   Ability to see the effects of the wrong on the other person

   Ability to empathize with those effects and be truly sorry for the other person as opposed to just feeling guilty

   Motivation to repent and change

   Ability to sustain repentance and change

   Commitment to a path of growth, a system of growth, and the involvement of other people in the growth process

   Ability to receive and utilize forgiveness

---

Why is such a person who meets these criteria a good bet? And which traits do you need to develop?

3. A person of good character will still fail, but generally they have "yellow light" sins that you can live with—as long as the person sees these problems in himself or herself and deals with them. Look below at the list of things that will annoy you but won't kill you, things you could learn to accept in mild doses. Which areas can you work on in yourself?

   Disorganization

   Difficulty with opening up and being direct about feelings or hurts

   Tendencies toward performance orientation

   Tendencies toward wanting to appear strong and avoiding vulnerability

   Perfectionism

   Some attempts to control

   Avoidance of closeness

   Impatience

   Messiness

   Nagging

---

4. What do these items listed suggest to you about where you could grow in being accepting and supportive of a fellow sinner? Put differently, what do you see about your tendency to be judgmental or perfectionistic?

> None of us gets everything right in relationships, and as a result we all are somewhat of a pain to be with at times. That is normal. Also, since you have to date sinners, decide which sins you can live with, or at least work with.

**10 minutes**

## Let's Talk: Major Imperfections

> Participant's Guide page 65.

Not all imperfections are in the yellow category. Some are bright red—as in *stop!* Some sins are more damaging than others. As Jesus said clearly, there are "weightier" aspects of God's law, and those are the ones that destroy relationships and hurt people, things like the lack of justice, mercy, and faithfulness (see Matthew 23:23). We're going to consider that category of character traits. Please turn to page 65.

### Directions

Pair up with a person near you and read through the questions on pages 65–67. You will have 10 minutes to complete this exercise. Any questions?

> Let the participants know when there is 1 minute remaining. Call the group back together after 10 minutes.

**6 minutes**

## Video Segment 2: "Beware When Opposites Attract"

The question "Whom should we date?" is a big one! We need to consider minor imperfections and major sins in the people we date. But we should also consider those imperfections and sins in ourselves if we are to be people worth dating. And then there's another important issue to think about in the *who* of dating. Dr. Townsend and Dr. Cloud will address that issue in our next video segment.

> Remind the participants that key points from the video segment can be found on page 68 of the Participant's Guide if they would like to review them at a later time.

> View Video Segment 2: "Beware When Opposites Attract."

Mature couples aren't too concerned about opposite traits. Instead, mature individuals are attracted by a person's ability to love, to forgive, to be honest, to be responsible, and to genuinely live the spiritual life. That kind of attraction is based on values, not on what you don't have inside but the other person does. Attraction based on oppositeness is not as strong a foundation for a relationship.

But opposites do attract. Let's look at why. Please turn to page 69.

---

## LET'S TALK
### *Major Imperfections*

**DIRECTIONS**

Pair up with a person near you and read through the questions found below. You will have 10 minutes to complete this exercise.

1. Character begins with yourself. In Psalm 101:2–8, David lists things he decided to avoid: faithlessness, perversity, evil, slander, pride, deceit, and wickedness. What can we do to build character in ourselves, godly character that is devoid of the traits David listed? What are *you* doing to build godly character?

2. Consider now some *personal* traits that are destructive to relationships.

   ***Destructive Personal Traits***

   Acts like he has it all together instead of admitting weakness and imperfection

   Is religious instead of spiritual

   Is defensive instead of open to feedback

   Is self-righteous instead of humble

   Apologizes instead of changes

   Avoids working on problems

   Demands trust instead of proving himself trustworthy

   Lies instead of telling the truth

   Is stagnant and not growing

   Is an addict

   Is duplicitous

---

When have you seen someone hurt (or been hurt yourself) by someone acting out one or more of these traits?

Which traits listed point out areas in which you could be growing?

3. Consider the following *interpersonal* traits that are destructive to relationships:

   ***Destructive Interpersonal Traits***

   Avoids closeness

   Thinks only about himself instead of the relationship and the other person

   Is controlling and resists freedom (in dating, this includes not respecting your limits in the physical realm)

   Flatters

   Condemns

   Plays "one up" or acts parental

   Is unstable over time

   Is a negative influence

   Gossips

   Is overly jealous and suspicious

   Negates pain

   Is overly angry

   When have you seen someone hurt (or been hurt yourself) by someone acting on one or more of these traits?

---

Which traits listed are areas in which you could be growing?

4. There are four steps to take if you find yourself in a dating relationship with someone who has a pattern of these destructive personal and/or interpersonal traits. They are the same as the steps to take if your date is not being truthful.

   1. Confront the problem directly.
   2. See what kind of response you get.
   3. Watch for a pattern of sustained repentance, change, and follow-through in growth.
   4. Only trust again and keep going if these "red lights" are no longer problems.

   Why would a support system be helpful, if not crucial, for someone needing to take these steps?

   Who in your support system can help you stand strong if and when you need to take these steps?

---

## VIDEO SEGMENT
### *Beware When Opposites Attract*

- The idea of complementary gifts and strengths is good for us emotionally, in more than one way. We have to learn humility to ask people for what we don't possess, and that helps us grow. We also can grow from the competencies of others.

- We should use and appreciate the abilities of those who have what we don't. However, the danger occurs when we make opposing styles or abilities a *basis* for relationship.

- Opposite-driven relationships often confuse dependency with true love.

- In mature couples, opposite traits are simply not a major issue. The two people are not drawn to opposite traits due to their own deficits; they are drawn to the values they share, such as love, responsibility, forgiveness, honesty, and spirituality.

- Attraction based on values is much more mature than attraction based on what you don't have inside.

- Immature couples seem to struggle more with finding someone who possesses the nurturance, structure, competence, or personality that they don't. Ultimately, they are looking for a parent to take care of part of them that they aren't taking care of in themselves.

- Make oppositeness a nonissue. Look more for character, love, and values than for which one of you has which qualities.

*10 minutes*

## Let's Talk: Why Opposites Attract

Participant's Guide page 69.

### Directions

Form groups of three or four and discuss the questions on pages 69–71. The italicized questions are for you to consider on your own as part of this week's "Boundary Building" exercise. Please disregard those at this time. You will have 10 minutes for this exercise. Any questions?

Let the participants know when there is 1 minute remaining. Call the group back together after 10 minutes.

Note: If time allows, you may want to have a follow-up discussion after the group has come back together.

## 2 MINUTES    SUMMARY

We've covered a lot of ground in considering the question "Whom should I be dating?" We've been challenged to learn the difference between human imperfections that everyone has and character flaws that are seriously damaging to a relationship. We need to learn to accept the person and deal with the minor problems, and not allow small things to ruin a relationship, but we also need to learn what imperfections are not benign, but are destructive. These "red light" imperfections should be a sign that the relationship itself is destructive. We are to confront those issues and trust someone again only when there is ownership and change.

We also learned to beware of being consistently attracted to our opposite. We need to make oppositeness a nonissue by looking more for character, love, and values than which person has which quality. Each of us needs to date someone who calls us into love, growth, and God—and then appreciate the unique differences between us.

To close, if you are feeling a lot of bad things as a result of being with a person—not simply the pain that comes from having a relationship, but injurious pain—let that be a sign. Protect yourself by knowing what you feel and value, and have the courage to stick to what you value for your dating life. Ultimately, you will get what you value. Look for godly character, value good things, and say no to things that destroy.

# PLANNING NOTES

_____

_____

_____

_____

_____

_____

_____

_____

_____

_____

_____

---

### LET'S TALK
#### *Why Opposites Attract*

**DIRECTIONS**

Form groups of three or four and discuss the questions below. The italicized questions are for you to consider on your own as part of this week's "Boundary Building" exercise. Please disregard those at this time. You will have 10 minutes to complete this exercise.

What is it about their opposites that people find so attractive? Why are we attracted to our opposite? There are several answers to this question.

**We do not want to work at developing ourselves.** The essence of the opposite issue is not really about the other person. It is about using another person to avoid dealing with our own souls.

1. Why is this an unhealthy motive for dating?

2. *When have you or someone you know piggybacked on another person's strengths instead of addressing an area of growth that needed work?*

**We want to be complete.** We are drawn to those who possess what we do not, so that we can internalize and own that trait for ourselves.

3. Why is dating not a good arena in which to develop oneself in a specific and important aspect of growth?

4. *When has a mentor, teacher, counselor, or friend helped you develop a character trait? Be specific about the process and how you benefited.*

---

**We are afraid of dealing with our deficits.** Another reason opposites attract is our fear of looking at our own character flaws. Self-exploration and change can be scary.

5. How might the following fears play themselves out in dating—making mistakes and failing; risking making others angry; having others leave us; guilt over hurting others; reexperiencing a painful past; looking at parts of ourselves that we don't like to see?

6. *Which of these have been or are issues for you? How, if at all, have those fears played themselves out in your dating life?*

7. *What role can a support group or a safe friend play in helping you deal with your fear?*

**We are spiritually lazy.** It is simply easier to have others do for us what we don't want to do for ourselves. This is the nature of immaturity, or "spiritual laziness." Such immaturity is the rageaholic who has to have his girlfriend soothe him when he is angry rather than learning to self-soothe and deal with his rage. The impulsive shopper depends on her boyfriend to untangle her finances. The introverted man looks to his girlfriend to maintain the relationships he should be developing.

8. These examples of immaturity show people failing to take ownership for what they lack and continuing to demand that others provide it. Which scenario, if any, have you seen or lived out yourself?

9. *Whether the problem is fear or laziness, we need to deal with our own deficits instead of looking to a date to heal them.*

---

*What role could a support group or a safe friend play in helping you with your laziness and irresponsibility?*

**We rely on our partner's gifts rather than dealing with our character deficits.** Sometimes the problem can be a confusion between giftedness and character deficits.

10. Consider three gauges of a healthy dating relationship where giftedness and ability are appreciated, but the two people still take ownership of their lives. First, each person deals with his own problems as his. It isn't the other's failure if we fail in an area we aren't strong in. Second, both members love and appreciate the gifts of the other person. However, they see the other's gifts as gifts, not as necessities to the relationship. Third, each member is actively involved in pursuing spiritual completion and growth in his areas of weakness.

11. What invitations to personal growth do you find in these statements?

12. *Do you find yourself continually needing to go to your date for things you should be doing for yourself—or do you see that pattern in your past? What are or were those "things"?*

The italicized questions in "Why Opposites Attract" as well as some additional questions about preferences are your "Boundary Building" exercise for this week. Now let's close in prayer.

**1 minute**          ## *Closing Prayer*

Lord God, thank you that you want to direct our paths, including our path through the world of dating. As you guide us to people to date, protect us from destructive relationships. Work in us to change any destructive ways in us, and give us the wisdom we need to recognize yellow and red lights in people's character. Give us both the patience we need for living with yellow-light sinners and boldness to take a stand and say no to the red-light things we shouldn't tolerate in a relationship. And convict us of our sin so that you can bring us to repentance and transform us.

As you're working on our character, please develop those areas in which we are weak. Help us to recognize our character deficits and then to look to you for growth rather than to a date for a sense of completion or wholeness. Help us to see with discernment a person's character rather than what strengths might complement our weaknesses. We pray all this in Jesus' name. Amen.

# PLANNING NOTES

_____

_____

_____

_____

_____

_____

_____

_____

_____

_____

_____

_____

_____

## Boundary Building

This week, work on the italicized questions in "Why Opposites Attract." Also take the time to answer the questions below about some important preferences. Answering these questions will help you build and maintain healthy boundaries for choosing whom you date.

### *Important Preferences*

**Common Interests**

What do you enjoy doing? Think about how you spend your free time and the activities that give you energy and joy.

Where are you going or could you go to meet people who share your top two or three interests?

**Common Goals**

What goals do you have for yourself? You may find it easier to think about where you'd like to be in five years, in ten, and in twenty-five.

Where are you going or could you go to meet people who are pursuing similar goals?

**Common Values**

What traits do you especially value in a person's character? Be as specific as possible.

When, if ever, have you compromised your standards regarding a person's character? Why did you do that? What might keep you from making that mistake again?

To search for character that shows the fruit of the Spirit—love, patience, kindness, and so forth (Galatians 5:22–23)—would be a good dating goal. Where might you undertake that search?

## Suggested Reading

For more thoughts on this session's topic, read chapters 6 and 9 in *Boundaries in Dating*: "What You Can Live With and What You Can't Live With" and "Beware When Opposites Attract." For a more thorough self-evaluation, look at chapters 6 and 9 in the *Boundaries in Dating Workbook*.

_____

_____

_____

_____

_____

_____

_____

_____

_____

_____

_____

_____

_____

# Session Six

# Whom Should I Be Dating? Part 2

## BEFORE YOU LEAD

### Key Points

- Many singles fall in love with someone they wouldn't be friends with.
- If you are attracted to someone who does not possess the character and friendship qualities that you need in a long-term relationship, do not think you are going to change him or her. If this is your pattern, see it as a problem, not simply a matter of not yet having found "the right one."
- Do everything possible to get to know the person you're attracted to. Can you share all of your values? Is the spiritual commitment the same? Are there character traits you find yourself ignoring, denying, or excusing? In short, would you pick this person as a friend?
- Find an accountability system to hold you to the boundary of not letting yourself go too far into a relationship with someone you would not be friends with. The best boundary you can have in your dating life is to begin every relationship with an eye toward friendship.
- "Romanticizing a friendship" refers to making friends into something they are not. Romantic feelings come from an idealization of the other person. This idealization can be caused by several things, both healthy and unhealthy.
- In a struggling relationship, one person can develop romantic feelings for the other out of his or her own neediness. This neediness becomes "romanticized," that is, it disguises its true nature in romance. This kind of romanticization can ruin a perfectly good friendship.
- Romanticization is often driven by the kind of loneliness that is a chronic, longstanding sense of emptiness in life, no matter what the circumstances. This loneliness is an indication that something is broken in one's soul, and it needs to be repaired through God's healing process, not by a friendship-turned-romantic.

## *Synopsis*

Sam sounded like he was "in love" with Kim, but he had a more real relationship with Stephanie. Stephanie had the deep connection and ability to share things that matter, communicate, and have fun with Sam, but Sam enjoyed the spark and chemistry with Kim. But he might be letting that chemistry blind him to some very important things that are essential for a good, lasting relationship. In short, he might be falling in love with a woman that he would not choose as a friend.

Many singles share Sam's problem. The person they are attracted to is not able to connect with all areas of their life, or they are attracted to someone who is not good for them at all. Dr. Cloud and Dr. Townsend have six points for singles who have this problem of falling in love with someone they wouldn't be friends with.

First, if you are attracted to someone who does not possess the character and friendship qualities you need in a long-term relationship, do not think that you are going to change him or her.

Second, if this is your pattern, see it as a problem, not simply a matter of not yet having found "the right one."

Third, do everything possible to get to know the person to whom you're attracted. Can you share all of your values? Is the spiritual commitment the same? Are there character traits you find yourself ignoring, denying, or excusing? In short, would you pick this person as a friend?

Fourth, are you confusing longing for being "in love"? Many times people long for a certain kind of fantasy person and think that this deep longing is being in love.

Fifth, are you confusing infatuation with love? Remember the phrase "in fat you ate." Infatuation is very similar to high-fat fast food—no lasting nutritional value!

Finally, and most important, find an accountability system to hold you to the boundary of not letting yourself go too far into a relationship with someone that you would not be friends with. Say no to letting your heart get involved with a person whom you would not choose as a friend. The best boundary you can have in your dating life is to begin every relationship with an eye toward friendship.

In this session, Dr. Cloud and Dr. Townsend also warn against ruining a friendship out of loneliness. Much good can come from healthy opposite-sex relationships, and much grief can be spared by not pursuing a romantic relationship when the feelings were simply not there. "Romanticizing a friendship" refers to making friends into something they are not. Romantic feelings come from an idealization of the other person. This idealization can be caused by several things, both healthy and unhealthy.

In a new relationship, each person knows little about the other person. Idealization fills in the gaps with good things in order to keep the couple involved in the relationship, and helps them tolerate the early parts of the developing connection. This is normal and expectable romanticization.

In a mature relationship, romantic idealization waxes and wanes. It arises out of a deep appreciation and gratitude for the person's presence and love, yet it retains the reality of who he or she is at the same time. This, too, is normal.

But in a struggling relationship one person can develop romantic feelings for the other out of his or her own neediness. This neediness becomes "romanticized"; that is, it disguises its true nature in romance. The person feels alive, driven, and motivated to be with the other. Yet the need is generally caused by some emptiness inside. This kind of romanticization is driven by loneliness and can ruin a perfectly good friendship.

Dr. Townsend and Dr. Cloud aren't talking about the loneliness that comes for a salesman on a long business trip who feels lonely for his support network while he's on the road and who takes steps to reconnect when he returns. They're talking about the loneliness that is a problem condition. The person can be around many loving, caring people, and still feel isolated. She may either feel that others don't care or that she is unable to receive what they give. This loneliness is an indication that something is broken in one's soul, something that needs to be repaired in God's healing process, not by a friendship-turned-romantic.

## Recommended Reading

"Don't Fall in Love with Someone You Wouldn't Be Friends With" and "Don't Ruin a Friendship out of Loneliness," chapters 7 and 8 of *Boundaries in Dating*

# Session Six

# Whom Should I Be Dating? Part 2

| | |
|---|---|
| **3 MINUTES** | **INTRODUCTION** |

| | |
|---|---|
| *1 minute* | ### Welcome |

> Call the group together and welcome the participants to Session 6, "Whom Should I Be Dating? Part 2."

| | |
|---|---|
| *1 minute* | ### Opening Prayer |

Thank you, Lord, for all you've taught us about dating and all you've shown us about ourselves as we've met together. We ask you to bless our time together now as we continue to seek your guidance in our dating life. Help us to learn more about whom you would have us date—and then help us to obey what you teach us. In Jesus' name. Amen.

| | |
|---|---|
| *1 minute* | ### Review and Overview |

> Participant's Guide page 73.

As we saw last time—and as we know from experience—the simple-sounding question "Whom should I be dating?" has no simple answer. We need to focus on a person's character more than on external traits, and we need to know what character traits are yellow lights and which are red. Put differently, we need to know what character traits we can live with and which ones we can't. We also need to understand what's usually going on when opposites attract. Then, with that understanding, we can work on making "who has what" and oppositeness nonissues and instead look at a person's character and values.

Let's turn to page 73.

# PLANNING NOTES

_____

_____

_____

_____

_____

_____

_____

_____

_____

_____

_____

_____

*Session Six*

# Whom Should I Be Dating? Part 2

## OVERVIEW

In this session you will

- Recognize the pointlessness and potential pain of falling in love with someone you wouldn't be friends with.
- Learn what to do if falling in love with someone you wouldn't be friends with is your pattern.
- Be warned against romanticizing a friendship.
- Discover various causes of such romanticization.
- Explore your loneliness to see if it is the normal need for connectedness or a sign of an injury that needs to be healed.

73

_____

_____

_____

_____

_____

_____

_____

_____

_____

_____

_____

_____

_____

_____

→ In this session we're going to continue to consider whom we should be dating. This time the focus will be on understanding the differences between friendships and dating relationships. We will learn to recognize the pointlessness and potential pain of falling in love with someone you wouldn't be friends with. We will determine what to do if falling in love with someone we wouldn't be friends with is a pattern. We will be warned against romanticizing a friendship and discover various causes of such romanticization. And we will explore loneliness to see if it is the normal need for connectedness or a sign of an injury that needs to be healed.

Let's start our session with a video entitled "Don't Fall in Love with Someone You Wouldn't Be Friends With."

## 47 MINUTES  DISCOVERY

**6 minutes**

### *Video Segment 1: "Don't Fall in Love with Someone You Wouldn't Be Friends With"*

> Remind the participants that key points from the video segment can be found on page 74 of their Participant's Guide if they would like to review them at a later time.

> View Video Segment 1: "Don't Fall in Love with Someone You Wouldn't Be Friends With."

Why is it good advice to not fall in love with someone you wouldn't want to be friends with?

> If this question alone doesn't generate discussion, try these prompts: "What characteristics of a friend would make that person good to fall in love with?" "Why would you settle for less?" or "What characteristics of a friend are important in a date or a spouse?"

Dr. Cloud and Dr. Townsend have written other books that can help you work through the kinds of issues that cause you to be attracted to the wrong kind of person. Those titles are *Safe People, Changes That Heal,* and *Hiding from Love.* The main point here is that you need to have some good boundaries with yourself in terms of allowing yourself to get further into relationship with someone you would not want to be friends with.

Let's take some time now to consider what causes people—and you may be one of them—to be attracted to the wrong kind of person.

# PLANNING NOTES

_____

_____

_____

_____

_____

_____

_____

_____

_____

_____

_____

_____

_____

_____

_____

_____

_____

_____

_____

_____

_____

_____

_____

_____

_____

**Session Six**

**Whom Should I Be Dating? Part 2**

### OVERVIEW

In this session you will

- Recognize the pointlessness and potential pain of falling in love with someone you wouldn't be friends with.
- Learn what to do if falling in love with someone you wouldn't be friends with is your pattern.
- Be warned against romanticizing a friendship.
- Discover various causes of such romanticization.
- Explore your loneliness to see if it is the normal need for connectedness or a sign of an injury that needs to be healed.

73

74      *Boundaries in Dating Paticipant's Guide*

### VIDEO SEGMENT

**Don't Fall in Love with Someone You Wouldn't Be Friends With**

- Many singles fall in love with someone they wouldn't be friends with. Perhaps you do too.
- If you are attracted to someone who does not possess the character and friendship qualities you need in a long-term relationship, do not think you are going to change him or her. If this is your pattern, see it as a problem, not simply a matter of not yet having found "the right one."
- Do everything possible to get to know the person you're attracted to. Can you share all of your values? Is the spiritual commitment the same? Are there character traits you find yourself ignoring, denying, or excusing? In short, would you pick this person as a friend?
- Are you confusing longing for being "in love"? Are you confusing infatuation with love?
- Find an accountability system to hold you to the boundary of not letting yourself go too far into a relationship with someone you would not be friends with. Say no to letting your heart get involved with a person whom you would not choose as a friend.
- The best boundary that you can have in your dating life is to begin every relationship with an eye toward friendship.

## *10 minutes*   *On Your Own: Reasons for Unhealthy Attraction*

> Participant's Guide page 75.

### Directions

Turn to pages 75–77 and answer the questions found there. What you don't finish will be part of this week's "Boundary Building" exercise. You will have 10 minutes for this exercise. Any questions?

> Let the participants know when there is 1 minute remaining. Call the group back together after 10 minutes.

Now that you've looked at some reasons why people (and maybe why you yourself) are attracted to the wrong kind of person, to someone they wouldn't be friends with, let's consider why friendship is so important. Please turn to page 78.

## *10 minutes*   *Let's Talk: The Path of Friendship*

> Participant's Guide page 78.

Romance is great. Sexuality is great. Attraction is great. But here is the key: *If all of those are not built upon lasting friendship and respect for the person's character, something is wrong.*

Since friendship is key to dating and marriage relationships, let's take a moment to consider what characteristics of a friend are important in a date or spouse.

> Take a few minutes to brainstorm a list of characteristics of a friend. Have the participants write down each trait in the space provided on page 78 of the Participant's Guide. Once the list is done, ask the group to eliminate any traits that are *un*important in a date. They shouldn't cross any traits off the list! Let this exercise underscore the fact that we shouldn't fall in love with someone we wouldn't be friends with.

### Directions

Pair up with a person near you and answer the questions found on page 78. You will have 6 minutes to do this exercise. Any questions?

> Let the participants know when there is 1 minute remaining. Call the group back together after 6 minutes.

## ON YOUR OWN
### Reasons for Unhealthy Attraction

**DIRECTIONS**

Answer the questions below. (What you don't finish will be part of this week's "Boundary Building" exercise.) You will have 10 minutes for this exercise.

**Unresolved family-of-origin issues.** If you had problems in the family you grew up in, those problems may surface in your dating relationships. One woman was attracted to a person who was like a parent she had struggled with. Another was attracted to someone who was the diametrical opposite of the hurtful parent.

1. What unresolved family-of-origin issues, if any, might surface in your dating relationships? What could you do to resolve those issues before they interfere?

**Unintegrated parts of yourself.** Another prime reason you may be attracted to people who would not be good for you is that you are looking to resolve some aspect of yourself you have never faced. Often if you do not possess a certain quality, you are drawn to someone who possesses it in the extreme. Sometimes a person is attracted to a bad thing: a "saint" falls head over heals with a "sinner." And sometimes a person has a pain or hurt she has never faced and is drawn to someone who has a lot of pain and problems.

2. When, if ever, have you seen or perhaps experienced for yourself one of these three scenarios? Whatever is in your heart is what you are going to find yourself dealing with, in one way or another, as you date. What can you do to guard your heart (Proverbs 4:23) and make it healthy so you will not be attracted to the wrong kinds of people?

**Defensive hope.** Have you had a lot of disappointment and loss in your life? If so, it may be difficult for you to let go of things, even things that are not good. You may have developed a pattern of "defensive hope": your hope that a date will change is a defense against the loss that would come with letting go of the relationship.

3. If you've ever been in this kind of situation, describe that experience and what you were thinking and feeling as you chose to stay in the unhealthy relationship. What would you say to someone in a similar situation today? What might help that person realize that the grief of letting go would not swallow him up?

**Romanticizing.** A "hopeless romantic" may be vulnerable to charmers who don't have the underlying character to carry on a lasting relationship. "Charm is deceptive" (Proverbs 31:30), and charmers and their prey are unable to get past romanticizing to real intimacy. If you have a tendency to romanticize everything, then you are avoiding the reality of what is going on. And the reality is what you are going to have to live with.

4. Do you describe yourself as a "hopeless romantic"? Do you have a long-standing Cinderella complex ("Someday my prince will come")? (Men can also have similar romantic feelings to the Cinderella complex.) Or are your fantasies a defense against depression or other kinds of disappointments? What can you do or who can you talk to to get a handle on what your romanticism is all about?

**Undeveloped intimacy.** Some people have never been connected with and known at a very deep level. At the most vulnerable parts of their heart, they have never been related to, so they don't know what real connection and intimacy is.

5. Are you aware of your undeveloped ability to be intimate? Does your dating history suggest that your detachment has been drawn to detachment? If you answer yes to either of these questions, what step toward a cure will you make? Specifically, what healing relationships—that are not romantic in nature—will you invest in so that all of your parts can be related to and find connection?

## LET'S TALK
### The Path of Friendship

**CHARACTERISTICS OF A FRIEND**

_____

_____

_____

_____

_____

_____

**DIRECTIONS**

Pair up with a person near you and answer the questions found below. You will have 6 minutes to do this exercise.

1. Think about lasting relationships you know of. What evidence do you see that each is built on friendship first?

2. The best boundary you can have in your dating life is to begin every relationship with an eye toward friendship. What does this advice mean in terms of what you do with a person in the early stages of a relationship? Put differently, what kinds of activities would help you see whether that person could be a friend?

3. Why should people not believe their feelings in the early stages of a possible dating relationship?

You want your best friends to be honest, faithful, deep, spiritual, responsible, connecting, growing, loving, and the like. Make sure that those qualities are also present in the person you are falling in love with.

As Dr. Cloud and Dr. Townsend have said, don't fall in love with someone you wouldn't be friends with—but, at the same time, don't ruin a good friendship by trying to make it more than it is or should be. That's the topic of our second video, "Don't Ruin a Friendship out of Loneliness."

**6 minutes**

## *Video Segment 2: "Don't Ruin a Friendship out of Loneliness"*

> Remind the participants that key points from the video segment can be found on page 79 of their Participant's Guide if they would like to review them at a later time.

> View Video Segment 2: "Don't Ruin a Friendship out of Loneliness."

So, romanticizing a friendship is not a good idea. Avoiding that mistake will be easier if we understand what causes romanticizing. Please turn to page 80.

**10 minutes**

## *Let's Talk: What Causes Romanticizing?*

> Participant's Guide page 80.

### Directions

1. Form groups of three or four.
2. Turn to pages 80–82 and answer the questions found there.
3. The questions in italics will be part of this week's "Boundary Building" exercise. Please disregard them for now.
4. You will have 10 minutes for this exercise. Any questions?

> Let the participants know when there is 1 minute remaining. Call the group back together after 10 minutes.

As we've talked about the dangers of ruining a friendship by romanticizing it, and why that romantic idealization happens, maybe you're wondering how you can know if a relationship is a friendship or a romance. Let's turn to page 83 to find out.

## VIDEO SEGMENT

### *Don't Ruin a Friendship out of Loneliness*

- Much good can come from healthy opposite-sex relationships, and much grief can be spared by not pursuing a romantic relationship when the feelings are simply not there.

- "Romanticizing a friendship" refers to making friends into something they are not.

- Romantic feelings come from an idealization of the other person.

- In a new relationship, each person knows little about the other person. Idealization fills in the gaps with good things in order to keep the couple involved in the relationship, and helps them tolerate the early parts of the developing connection.

- In a mature relationship, romantic idealization waxes and wanes. It arises out of a deep appreciation and gratitude for the person's presence and love, yet it retains the reality of who he or she is at the same time.

- In a struggling relationship, one person can develop romantic feelings for the other out of his or her own neediness. This neediness becomes "romanticized"; that is, it disguises its true nature in romance. This kind of romanticization is driven by loneliness, by a chronic, longstanding sense of emptiness in life, no matter what the circumstances.

- This loneliness is an indication that something is broken in one's soul, and needs to be repaired by God's healing process, not by a friendship-turned-romantic.

## LET'S TALK

### *What Causes Romanticizing?*

**DIRECTIONS**

1. Form groups of three or four.
2. Answer the questions found below.
3. The questions in italics will be part of this week's "Boundary Building" exercise. Please disregard them for now.
4. You will have 10 minutes for this exercise.

**Conflicts in experiencing dependency.** People who romanticize often are unable to feel their dependency for what it is: dependency. Fear of the depth of the internal emptiness; feeling bad as well as lonely; being ashamed of feeling needy; afraid to risk reaching out for fear of being hurt; feeling helpless and powerless when they feel their needs—these are some reasons people are unable to feel their dependency.

1. What are some healthy responses to feeling lonely? To feeling dependent or needy?

2. *Are you unable to feel your dependency as dependency? If so, which, if any, of the five reasons listed may be behind that inability?*

**Failures in relating to the same sex.** Often, those who romanticize their friends have a history of not being able to safely and deeply connect to the same sex so they keep trying to have significant connection with members of the opposite sex.

3. Romanticizers have pre-adult needs such as the need for belonging, for being safe, and for feeling comforted and

loved. What can a person do to let God and safe nonromantic relationships meet those needs?

4. *Where, if at all, do you see yourself limited in your ability to connect with members of the same sex? Are you, for instance, worried that you will hurt the other person, do you doubt that they have anything to offer, do you have contempt for the stereotypical weaknesses of their gender, or do you fear that you will lose opposite-sex opportunities by spending time with same-sex friends? What will you do about any truth you realize about yourself here?*

**Idealizing romance.** Some people think that romance is the highest form of friendship. Many people who are "into" romance feel that friendship is a grade lower than a romance. Don't get caught in the idea that you are missing out by keeping your friend as "only" your friend.

5. Romantic relationships are not better than friendships. They are different and meet different needs. List some of the differences and some of the different needs that are met.

6. *When, if ever, have you thought that a romantic relationship is better than a friendship and tried to elevate the friendship? What happened to the friendship—and what did you learn from the experience?*

**Rescue/caretaking roles.** Sometimes people who get caught up in romanticizing have tendencies to get into certain ways of relating called *rescuing* and *caretaking*. The "rescuee" will signal a need for someone to take care of him. The "caretaker" will receive the signal and go support, comfort, or solve the problems of the rescuee.

7. Why is this an unhealthy dynamic in a dating relationship?

8. *When, if ever, have you fallen first into this pattern and then fallen in love with either your caretaker or the one you cared for?*

**Impulsiveness.** Some people struggle with romanticization because they have difficulty with their drives and impulses. They become sexually involved very quickly, or are into quick, intense, "deep" connections.

9. Why doesn't impulsive romanticization lead to satisfying relationships?

10. *When, if ever, have you or someone you know tried to take either of these shortcuts to a significant relationship? What happened?*

**5 minutes**  ## A Few More Thoughts on ... How to Know a Friendship from a Romance

Participant's Guide page 83.

Here are some ways to see if you are wrecking a friendship by romanticizing.

→ Get connected OUTSIDE of the relationship. We all need people who will love us, support us, and tell us the truth on a continual basis. The need to be connected with others cannot be overemphasized. In fact, until you are connected to others, your deep needs for relationship can distort your thinking and objectivity. If you aren't connected to others, you'll be navigating the waters of dating—and life!—alone, and that's not wise.

Evaluate the FRUITS of the relationship. True romance and a romanticized friendship are after very different goals. What do you value in the relationship?

Get FEEDBACK. Turn to one of your truth-telling friends for some input. Ask your friends if you are a romance addict. Also ask them to evaluate what kind of friend you are to them. Find out if they know the deeper parts of who you are.

| Healthy Romance | Romanticized Friendship |
|---|---|
| Desire is based on first being rooted in love elsewhere. | Desire is based on empty NEEDINESS for the other person. |
| Other's FREEDOM is valued. | Other's freedom is a problem. |
| Relationship DRAWS IN friends. | Relationship shuts others out. |
| Conflicts work out okay. | Conflicts THREATEN the relationship. |
| MUTUAL feelings. | One person feels romantic; the other doesn't. |
| Friendship and romantic feelings COEXIST. | All-friend or all-romantic feelings; can't be both at the same time. |

# PLANNING NOTES

_____

_____

_____

_____

_____

_____

_____

_____

_____

_____

_____

_____

_____

_____

### A FEW MORE THOUGHTS ON ...
### HOW TO KNOW A FRIENDSHIP FROM A ROMANCE

- Get connected _____ of the relationship.

- Evaluate the _____ of the relationship. True romance and a romanticized friendship are after very different goals.

- Get _____.

| Healthy Romance | Romanticized Friendship |
|---|---|
| Desire is based on first being rooted in love elsewhere. | Desire is based on empty _____ for the other person. |
| Other's _____ is valued. | Other's freedom is a problem. |
| Relationship _____ friends. | Relationship shuts others out. |
| Conflicts work out okay. | Conflicts _____ the relationship. |
| _____ feelings. | One person feels romantic; the other doesn't. |
| Friendship and romantic feelings _____. | All-friend or all-romantic feelings; can't be both at the same time. |

_____

_____

_____

_____

_____

_____

_____

_____

_____

_____

_____

_____

_____

## 2 MINUTES    SUMMARY

Today we've seen that friendship and shared values are the things that last in a relationship. If romance, sexuality, and attraction aren't built upon lasting friendship and respect of that person's character, something is wrong. Friendship should always be an underlying foundation of any romantic relationship. Romance is fleeting, but friendship lasts. Dr. Cloud and Dr. Townsend encourage us to become deeply involved in our friendships, valuing the good things we get out of them. This can fulfill you inside and help resolve the tendency to romanticize—and ruin—perfectly satisfying platonic relationships.

In order to avoid that tendency, take time this week to do the "Boundary Building" exercise on page 84. Finish "Unhealthy Attractions," do the italicized questions in "What Causes Romanticizing," and take time to use the "Healthy Romance/Romanticized Friendship" chart on page 83 to evaluate any current relationship you're wondering about. Now let's close in prayer.

## *1 minute*    *Closing Prayer*

Lord God, the advice "Don't fall in love with someone you wouldn't be friends with" sounds simple enough, but that doesn't mean it's easy to live out. Please help us to be honest about our relationships—honest before you, honest with ourselves, and honest with a close friend or two—so that we can avoid some of the heartache that dating can bring. Also, teach us to value friendship—a friendship rooted in you—as the underlying foundation of any romantic relationship.

And, in light of the fact that friendships can be ruined by romanticizing rooted in loneliness, we thank you that you have made us to be in relationship and that you make us to seek relationship. Help us first and always to seek connectedness with you. Teach us also to build and maintain safe, healthy friendships. Then, when it's time for romance, may we include you and our friends in the process so that the result is healthy romance, not romanticized friendship. In Jesus' name. Amen.

# PLANNING NOTES

## Boundary Building

This week, as you continue to think about whom you should be dating, finish "Reasons for Unhealthy Attraction," complete the italicized questions in "What Causes Romanticizing," and take time to use the "Healthy Romance/Romanticized Friendship" chart on page 83 to evaluate any current relationship you're wondering about.

## Suggested Reading

For more thoughts on this session's topic, read chapters 7 and 8 in *Boundaries in Dating*: "Don't Fall in Love with Someone You Wouldn't Be Friends With" and "Don't Ruin a Friendship out of Loneliness." For a more thorough self-evaluation, look at chapters 7 and 8 in the *Boundaries in Dating Workbook*.

# Session Seven

# Solving Dating Problems When You're Part of the Problem, Part 1

## BEFORE YOU LEAD

### Key Points

- It's better to find out early in a relationship that you are with someone who cannot adapt to your wishes than to find out much later or, God forbid, after marriage.
- Don't be someone you are not just to gain a person's love. If you do, the person your loved one is loving is not you, but the role you are playing.
- You cannot go through life without pursuing your own wishes, needs, and desires—nor should you. Your needs and desires are going to come out, and you had better find out early in the relationship how the person you are dating will deal with sometimes having to adapt to you.
- The problem of premature commitment and overinvolvement in a dating relationship ("too much, too fast") is a common one.
- Dating for a year, not including the engagement period, is a good minimum. When you date for at least a year, you experience the rhythm of life and a wide variety of experiences, including holidays, fiscal periods, vacations, and school terms. You can see how the relationship weathers the flow of both people's lives.
- Many things, including loneliness, difficulty in leaving home, difficulties in sustaining friendships, and perfectionism, contribute to couples seeing time as an adversary.
- If your dating relationships tend to move too quickly, consider that a signal and ask yourself why. Make sure you're not moving quickly because you are avoiding some other pain, such as loneliness or inner hurt.

- Real love takes time and has no shortcut, but it is worth it. Ask God to make you patient with the process of love so that you will be able to experience its growth day by day.

## *Synopsis*

If you try to be someone you are not just to gain a person's love, that person is not loving you, but the role you are playing. You cannot go through life without pursuing your own wishes, needs, and desires—nor should you. Your needs and desires are going to come out, and you had better find out early in the relationship how the person you are dating will deal with sometimes having to adapt to you.

The first lesson in this session is to be yourself from the beginning. If you are a real person from the start, a relationship of mutuality has a chance of developing. If you are not, then you might be headed for trouble.

A second important lesson in this session is hinted at in the phrase "too much, too fast." The problem of premature commitment and overinvolvement in a dating relationship is a common one. Two people find they have strong feelings for each other. They quickly begin investing enormous amounts of time in the relationship, neglecting other people, interests, and activities. The couple is typified by a drivenness to become highly committed, a process that takes less than a normal amount of time.

And what is normal? The Bible is not explicit, but Dr. Cloud and Dr. Townsend suggest that a year, not including the engagement period, is a good minimum. When you date for at least a year, you experience the rhythm of life and a wide variety of experiences, including holidays, fiscal periods, vacations, and school terms. It allows you to see how the relationship weathers the flow of both people's lives.

Yet many people meet, date, and mate within a few months or even weeks. They believe they have recognized the right person and think they are ready for marriage. Or some couples will take the requisite year or two to date, but will have a problem in "frontloading" the relationship: they become deeply committed very soon in the game, and never go through a process of gradually becoming closer over time. Couples like these see time as an adversary. What contributes to this view?

Among the many reasons is loneliness. Loneliness is one of the most painful yet necessary experiences in life. People feel incomplete, empty, or even starving inside. Loneliness can make people do almost anything to fill up the hole inside—including rush a relationship. Don't. Instead, use your loneliness as a signal to get connected with some good, solid, nondating relationships.

Second, some couples "couple" quickly because they have not finished the task of emotionally leaving home. They are unable to navigate the single life. They are still emotionally dependent on their family of origin and are at some level yearning for a home environment they never finished leaving. So they opt more for the marriage state than the other person.

Third, some people overcommit due to problems making deep and lasting friendships. They find it hard to get truly close to people, and instead of developing a good community, they choose one romantic relationship on which to focus.

Fourth, perfectionism can cause people to commit too quickly. You might think that, being too picky, perfectionists would never marry. But some perfectionists become quickly committed to a person who seems to represent every weakness they don't have. Their friends may scratch their heads in bewilderment, but that person, being unable to resolve her own weaknesses, badness, and imperfections, falls in love with someone who possesses them. She does not face her own weaknesses, but focuses on the other's.

If your dating relationships tend to move too quickly, consider that a signal and ask yourself why. Make sure you're not moving quickly because you are avoiding some other pain, such as loneliness or inner hurt. Quick, intense relationships often end up either burning out or being shallow. Real love takes time and has no shortcut, but it is worth it. Ask God to make you patient with the process of love so that you will be able to experience its growth day by day.

## Recommended Reading

"Adapt Now, Pay Later" and "Too Much, Too Fast," chapters 10 and 11 of *Boundaries in Dating*

# *Session Seven*

# Solving Dating Problems When You're Part of the Problem, Part 1

| | |
|---|---|
| **3 MINUTES** | **INTRODUCTION** |
| *1 minute* | **Welcome** |

> Call the group together and welcome the participants to Session 7, "Solving Dating Problems When You're Part of the Problem, Part 1."

*1 minute* **Opening Prayer**

Lord God, you are holy, you are perfect, and you don't make mistakes. But we, whom you created, are very different. We sin, we are far from perfect, we make mistakes, and we bring problems on ourselves. During this session help us to see ourselves with open eyes so that we can learn how to solve some problems in dating that arise because of us. We pray in Jesus' name. Amen.

*1 minute* **Review and Overview**

> Participant's Guide page 85.

We started this *Boundaries in Dating* series by spending four sessions on boundaries. We talked about why boundaries are important in dating and how honesty is an essential boundary. Then we thought about how to take God on a date and acknowledged that dating won't cure a lonely heart. We've also tried to learn from the past so that we

# PLANNING NOTES

---

*Session Seven*

# Solving Dating Problems When You're Part of the Problem, Part 1

## OVERVIEW

In this session you will

- Consider the consequences of adapting to your date's wishes, needs, and desires rather than also being honest about your own.

- Think about what, if anything, keeps you from being honest about who you are.

- Learn both the value of moving slowly in a dating relationship and some signs of moving too fast.

- Look at why you may move too fast in a dating relationship.

85

don't repeat mistakes we've made. After that, we spent two sessions considering whom we should be dating. And now we're going to start talking about how to solve common dating problems.

Let's turn to page 85.

→ This week we will consider the consequences of adapting to your date's wishes, needs, and desires rather than also being honest about your own. We will think about what, if anything, keeps you from being honest about who you are. We will also learn both the value of moving slowly in a dating relationship and some signs of moving too fast. And, finally, we will look at why you may move too fast in a dating relationship.

Let's get started.

# 45 MINUTES DISCOVERY

**6 minutes**

## *Video Segment 1: "Adapt Now, Pay Later"*

> Remind the participants that key points from the video segment can be found on page 86 of their Participant's Guide if they would like to review them at a later time.

> View Video Segment 1: "Adapt Now, Pay Later."

"Be yourself from the beginning." That wise advice sounds simple enough, but let's talk about whether or not it's easy to do. What warning can we take from Keri's experience?

> Solicit responses from the group. Possible answers include: "We need to be honest about who we are from the start"; "We need our friends to get to know our dates"; or "We need to learn how our date handles it when we disagree or have our own ideas."

How can healthy boundaries keep us from adapting too much, or put differently, how can they help us be honest about our wishes, needs, and desires?

> Solicit responses from the group. Encourage participants to share specific examples (real-life or hypothetical). Be sure to have some examples of your own to share. You might, for instance, talk about how the boundary of truth requires us to be honest about who we are, and that means being honest about what we like in music, church, movies, restaurants, and activities. Healthy boundaries can also enable us to die to self when we choose to and it's appropriate. Healthy boundaries help us allow differences in tastes to exist and even to add spice to a relationship.

# PLANNING NOTES

_____

_____

_____

_____

_____

_____

_____

_____

_____

_____

_____

_____

_____

_____

_____

_____

_____

_____

_____

_____

_____

_____

_____

---

*Session Seven*

# Solving Dating Problems When You're Part of the Problem, Part 1

## OVERVIEW

In this session you will

- Consider the consequences of adapting to your date's wishes, needs, and desires rather than also being honest about your own.

- Think about what, if anything, keeps you from being honest about who you are.

- Learn both the value of moving slowly in a dating relationship and some signs of moving too fast.

- Look at why you may move too fast in a dating relationship.

85

---

## VIDEO SEGMENT

### *Adapt Now, Pay Later*

- It's better to find out early in a relationship that you are with someone who cannot adapt to your wishes than to find out much later or, God forbid, after marriage.

- Don't be someone you are not just to gain a person's love. If you do, the person is not loving you, but the role you are playing.

- You cannot go through life without also pursuing your own wishes, needs, and desires—nor should you. Your needs and desires are going to come out, and you had better find out early in the relationship how the person you are dating will deal with sometimes having to adapt to you.

- Be yourself from the beginning. If you are a real person from the start, a relationship of mutuality has a chance of developing. If you are not, then you might be headed for trouble.

Thanks for sharing your thoughts. Let's take some time now to consider how adaptive you are in relationships. Please turn to page 87.

## *10 minutes*

# *On Your Own: Wishes, Needs, Desires*

> Participant's Guide page 87.

## Directions

On your own, work through the questions on pages 87–88. You will have 10 minutes to complete this exercise. Any questions?

> Let the participants know when there is 1 minute remaining. Call the group back together after 10 minutes.

## *6 minutes*

# *Video Segment 2: "Too Much, Too Fast"*

Adapting to our date's wishes, needs, and desires and keeping quiet about our own is only one way we can cause problems in our dating relationships. In this next video segment, Dr. Townsend and Dr. Cloud talk about another way. Let's hear what they have to say.

> Remind the participants that key points from the video segment can be found on page 89 of their Participant's Guide if they wish to review them at a later time.

> View Video Segment 2: "Too Much, Too Fast."

Dr. Townsend and Dr. Cloud discussed four reasons why people sometimes don't wait. Let's spend some time now discussing three benefits that come from waiting. Please turn to page 90.

## *18 minutes*

# *Let's Talk: Why Wait?*

> Participant's Guide page 90.

1. I will be dividing you into three groups and assigning each group one set of questions from pages 90–92.
2. Each group should choose a spokesperson.
3. You will have 10 minutes to go through your group's set of questions. As before, the italicized questions are part of your "Boundary Building" exercise. Please disregard them for now.
4. When I call the groups back together, I will ask each group's spokesperson to share their group's thoughts. Any questions?

## ON YOUR OWN
### *Wishes, Needs, Desires*

**DIRECTIONS**

Work through the following questions. You will have 10 minutes to complete this exercise.

An important lesson of this session is to *be yourself from the beginning,* and then you can find someone who is authentic as well.

1. What, if anything, keeps you from being yourself? What fears, past hurts, or daunting risks prompt you to be more compliant than may be healthy and wise?

2. Keri's friend Sandy helped her see reality and cope with the loss of Steve. What safe friend is close enough to see the dynamics of your dating relationship and whether you are really being yourself?

People who are selfish and controlling can only be that way if they are in relationship with someone who is adaptive. If someone stands up to them and is honest about his or her wants and desires, then the controlling person has to learn to share or gets frustrated and goes away.

3. If you tend to be adaptive, what is fueling that tendency and what can you do to heal the underlying hurt or meet the hidden need in a healthier way?

---

4. Similarly, what may be keeping you from being honest about wants and desires? And, again, what can you do to heal the underlying hurt or meet the hidden need in a healthier way?

A relationship between two authentic people has mutuality and partnership. It has give and take. It has equality. It has sharing and mutual self-sacrifice for the sake of the other and the relationship. If you are a real person from the start, a relationship of mutuality has a chance of developing.

---

## VIDEO SEGMENT
### *Too Much, Too Fast*

- The problem of premature commitment and overinvolvement in a dating relationship ("too much, too fast") is a common one.

- Dating for a year, not including the engagement period, is a good minimum. When you date for at least a year, you experience the rhythm of life and a wide variety of experiences, including holidays, fiscal periods, vacations, and school terms. You can see how the relationship weathers the flow of both people's lives.

- Many things, including loneliness, difficulty in leaving home, difficulties in sustaining friendships, and perfectionism, contribute to couples seeing time as an adversary.

- If your dating relationships tend to move too quickly, consider that a signal and ask yourself why. Make sure you're not moving quickly because you are avoiding some other pain, such as loneliness or inner hurt.

- Real love takes time and has no shortcut, but it is worth it. Ask God to make you patient with the process of love so that you will be able to experience its growth day by day.

---

## LET'S TALK
### *Why Wait?*

**DIRECTIONS**

1. The leader will divide you into three groups and assign each group one topic from below.
2. Each group should choose a spokesperson.
3. You will have 10 minutes to go through your group's topic. As before, the italicized questions are for you to answer at home as part of your "Boundary Building" exercise.
4. When the group is called back together, each group's spokesperson will be asked to share their group's thoughts.

Why should you wait, take time, and gradually become closer to a person to whom you are enormously attracted? Here are three answers to that question.

1. **Relationships do not tolerate shortcuts.** We have to understand the nature of relationships as God designed them. Relationships grow in a healthy manner only as they undergo experiences—and there is no shortcut to experiences. Consider these eight time-consuming dating activities:
   - Having enough talks to safely open up with each other
   - Entering each other's worlds of work, hobbies, worship, and service
   - Meeting and spending time with each other's friends
   - Understanding each other's strengths and weaknesses
   - Going over basic values and what is important in life to each other
   - Getting to know each other's families
   - Spending time away from each other to think through the relationship, both alone and with friends
   - Learning your best style of disagreement and conflict management

> Divide the participants into three groups and assign each a set of questions.

> Let the participants know when there is 1 minute remaining. Call the group back together after 10 minutes. Take 8 minutes to get reports from each of the three groups.

Now that we've talked about why we should wait, let me add a few more thoughts on going too fast.

**5 minutes**

## A Few More Thoughts on . . . Going Too Fast

> Participant's Guide page 93.

Please turn to page 93 and fill in the blanks as we go along.

### You Are Committing Too Quickly If . . .

It can be difficult to know you are going too fast. Love does have an individual pace for people. Some can safely progress more quickly than others. They may be better decision-makers or be more mature in relationships with others.

➔ Here are some ways of determining if you are committing too quickly:

- You "know" each other EMOTIONALLY more than you "know" each other OBJECTIVELY.
- You find yourself more INVESTED in the relationship than in areas of your life that are important to you.
- You abruptly STOP dating others.
- You get FEEDBACK from FRIENDS that this seems to be going quickly.

Whatever the signs, pay attention to them. As a rule of thumb, it is better to err on the side of caution.

### Slowing Down the Pace

➔ If your dating life tends to be too much, too fast, here are some tips to follow. These tips are not enjoyable, and they involve some work, but if you are tired of the roller coaster of intense but failed relationships, they are worth it.

- IDENTIFY what is driving the pace (loneliness, fear of being out in the world, problems in making friends, or perfectionism). Work on these issues.

## LET'S TALK
### *Why Wait?*

**DIRECTIONS**

1. The leader will divide you into three groups and assign each group one topic from below.

2. Each group should choose a spokesperson.

3. You will have 10 minutes to go through your group's topic. As before, the italicized questions are for you to answer at home as part of your "Boundary Building" exercise.

4. When the group is called back together, each group's spokesperson will be asked to share their group's thoughts.

Why should you wait, take time, and gradually become closer to a person to whom you are enormously attracted? Here are three answers to that question.

1. **Relationships do not tolerate shortcuts.** We have to understand the nature of relationships as God designed them. Relationships grow in a healthy manner only as they undergo experiences—and there is no shortcut to experiences. Consider these eight time-consuming dating activities:
   - Having enough talks to safely open up with each other
   - Entering each other's worlds of work, hobbies, worship, and service
   - Meeting and spending time with each other's friends
   - Understanding each other's strengths and weaknesses
   - Going over basic values and what is important in life to each other
   - Getting to know each other's families
   - Spending time away from each other to think through the relationship, both alone and with friends
   - Learning your best style of disagreement and conflict management

What is the value of each of these experiences? Why aren't shortcuts possible? (Could all this be done in a few short months?)

*When have you been surprised by who a person (friend, business associate, or date) really was once you got to know that person through shared experiences? Comment on what the shared experiences revealed that you hadn't known about that person before.*

2. **A measure of importance.** The time involved in dating someone should reflect the significance of the relationship. Simply put, the more important a decision is, the more time it should take to make it. Our most important human relationship should warrant the time due it.

   Read through the following list of some of the significant aspects of marriage:

   - A lifelong commitment to loving one person only
   - Forsaking all other opportunities for romantic love
   - Being in relationship with all the bad, immature, and broken parts of that person
   - Having your own bad, immature, and broken parts open to the scrutiny of that person
   - Solving conflict in ways that do not involve leaving the relationship
   - Staying in the relationship even if the other person changes for the worse
   - Being called to sacrifice many individual preferences for the sake of the relationship

Which of those serve as a wake-up call to the seriousness of marriage? What do these items suggest about the importance of not rushing the dating relationship?

*When, if ever, have you experienced loneliness within a relationship? How did that compare to being alone?*

3. **The nature of love.** Another reason to take your time is that this is a necessary part of learning how to love. Dating should not only produce a mate; it should also develop within you the ability to love that mate deeply and well. And love, as the Bible defines it, is a stance of working for the best for another person.

   Taking time in your dating relationship helps you clarify the distinction between need and love. What relationship have you've seen or perhaps been involved in that seemed propelled forward by one or more of needs listed below? Describe what happened.

   - Needing the security of knowing he has your total commitment

   - Wanting to end the sexual frustration that comes with singleness

   - Needing the relationship in order to feel complete

   - Needing someone to relate to in his life

*When has a friendship or dating relationship taught you something about how to love? Explain.*

## A FEW MORE THOUGHTS ON . . . GOING TOO FAST
### *You Are Committing Too Quickly If . . .*

- You "know" each other _____ more than you "know" each other _____.
- You find yourself more _____ in the relationship than in areas of your life that are important to you.
- You abruptly _____ dating others.
- You get _____ from _____ that this seems to be going quickly.

### *Slowing Down the Pace*

- _____ what is driving the pace (loneliness, fear of being out in the world, problems in making friends, or perfectionism). Work on those issues.
- Get a _____. A full life is probably the best antidote for getting too close, too fast. Ask God to help you get involved in real life: spending time on friends, work, hobbies, church, service, and God himself.
- Deliberately slow the pace to _____ the relationship. If the relationship is mature, it will withstand the test of slowing down.
- Investigate _____ is contributing to the pace. Does it tend to be _____, those you date, or both?
- Ask friends for _____. Humbly go to mature, safe friends and ask them to tell you when you're getting weird. Give them permission to tell you to _____!

- Get a LIFE. A full life is probably the best antidote for getting too close, too fast. Ask God to help you get involved in real life: spending time on friends, work, hobbies, church, service, and God himself.
- Deliberately slow the pace to DIAGNOSE the relationship. If the relationship is mature, it will withstand the test of slowing down.
- Investigate WHO is contributing to the pace. Does it tend to be YOU, those you date, or both?
- Ask friends for FEEDBACK. Humbly go to mature, safe friends and ask them to tell you when you're getting weird. Give them permission to tell you to STOP!

It is easy to get overcommitted quickly in the world of dating. However, resolving what is driving that pace can provide a more balanced and healthy dating life.

## 2 MINUTES     SUMMARY

Adapt now, pay later. Too much, too fast. There's a lot of wisdom behind those two phrases, and this week's "Boundary Building" exercise, found on page 94, can help you build on that wisdom. Please take some time this week to work through it.

Next time we'll look at how to solve three other dating problems that can arise when we're part of the problem. Right now, let's close in prayer.

## *1 minute*     *Closing Prayer*

Holy God, we've seen it again today: the importance of being truthful about who we are, about what we want and desire. As we take the risk of having someone know us, give us courage. And help us live in the light of truth in small ways as well as big ways.

We also ask you to help us trust enough in your good plans for us that we will move slowly in our relationships, taking time to seek your will, to hear the counsel of friends, to work on the issues we need to work on, and to learn to love as you would have us love. Then, Lord, when the time is right, make us patient with the process of love and able to experience and enjoy its growth day by day. We pray all this in Jesus' name. Amen.

# PLANNING NOTES

_____

_____

_____

_____

_____

_____

_____

_____

_____

_____

_____

_____

_____

_____

_____

_____

_____

_____

_____

_____

_____

_____

_____

_____

---

### A FEW MORE THOUGHTS ON . . . GOING TOO FAST

#### *You Are Committing Too Quickly If . . .*

- You "know" each other _____ more than you "know" each other _____.

- You find yourself more _____ in the relationship than in areas of your life that are important to you.

- You abruptly _____ dating others.

- You get _____ from _____ that this seems to be going quickly.

#### *Slowing Down the Pace*

- _____ what is driving the pace (loneliness, fear of being out in the world, problems in making friends, or perfectionism). Work on those issues.

- Get a _____. A full life is probably the best antidote for getting too close, too fast. Ask God to help you get involved in real life: spending time on friends, work, hobbies, church, service, and God himself.

- Deliberately slow the pace to _____ the relationship. If the relationship is mature, it will withstand the test of slowing down.

- Investigate _____ is contributing to the pace. Does it tend to be _____, those you date, or both?

- Ask friends for _____. Humbly go to mature, safe friends and ask them to tell you when you're getting weird. Give them permission to tell you to _____!

---

## Boundary Building

When, if ever, have you done more than the normal initial adapting in order not to jeopardize a developing relationship? When—and how—did you realize that things went smoothly only as long as you adapted to your date and that your date was unable to deal with your needs and desires?

Are you adapting now, only to pay later? Find out by evaluating yourself according to the following criteria:

1. Do you tell the truth about where you want to go and not go, or what you want to do or not do?
2. Are you honest about your preferences and desires?
3. Are you acting as if you like things that your date likes just so you will be accepted? Being liked for who you are requires that you be that person!
4. Are you afraid to share your desires and wants for fear of conflict?
5. Are you getting feedback from honest friends to see if you are really being yourself and if you are seeing the relationship realistically?

What do your answers tell you about whether you are adapting too much—and what are you going to do in light of what you've realized about yourself?

Also during the coming week, take some time to answer the italicized questions from the "Why Wait?" section and review the tips for slowing down a relationship found in "A Few More Thoughts on ... Going Too Fast." What do you need to do, if anything, to slow down the pace of your dating relationships?

## Suggested Reading

For more thoughts on this session's topic, read chapters 10 and 11 in *Boundaries in Dating:* "Adapt Now, Pay Later" and "Too Much, Too Fast." For a more thorough self-evaluation, look at chapters 10 and 11 in the *Boundaries in Dating Workbook*.

# *Session Eight*

# Solving Dating Problems When You're Part of the Problem, Part 2

## BEFORE YOU LEAD

### *Key Points*

- One aspect of safe dating is to remain connected to your friends and support system. By doing so, you'll make sure you are not vulnerable to what you cannot see on your own but would be able to see with the help of other people.
- We're part of a dating problem when we don't put boundaries on blame. Blaming is ascribing responsibility to someone for a fault.
- Blame helps differentiate between what is our fault and what is another's. The blame that kills a good dating relationship is when one person sees herself as blameless and attributes almost all of the problems in the relationship to the other person.
- Learn to humbly listen to correction and restrain the urge to react in blame. Be more concerned about your own soul's state than that of your date's.
- Accept what is negative about your date and work with the realities instead of staying locked in protest, argument, and blame. Finally, be a forgiver—and make mutual forgiveness a part of your dating relationships.
- To determine whether your hope for your dating relationship is merited, consider two truths. First, it is crazy to continue to do the same thing expecting different results. Second, the best predictor of the future, without some intervening variable, is the past.
- As you date, hope in God, hope in his principles, hope in people of trustworthy character, and hope in your own growth.

# Synopsis

A relationship that gets rid of one's individual life and friends, time, and space altogether is not a healthy relationship. Friends are an important space-giving freedom that will help you be healthier and more well-rounded. In addition, they will notice if you are losing them to a dating relationship and they'll let you know.

So work out your dating relationship with the help of your friends. If you are dating in a vacuum, you are in great danger. Stay connected, stay safe, and stay wise.

We're also part of the problem when we cling to false hope. To determine whether your hope for your dating relationship is merited, consider two truths. First, it is crazy to continue to do the same thing expecting different results. Second, the best predictor of the future, without some intervening variable, is the past. These two truths can help you determine whether your current hope is merited. Be honest with yourself.

As you date, hope in God, hope in his principles, hope in people of trustworthy character, and hope in your own growth. Those are truly good reasons for hope. But don't throw hope away on things which have no reality behind them.

Finally, we're part of a dating problem when we don't put boundaries on blame. Blame is ascribing responsibility to someone for a fault. When we accuse another of a problem, we are blaming. Blame is not bad in and of itself; it has a good function. However, the blame that kills a good dating relationship is when one person sees herself as blameless and attributes almost all of the problems in the relationship to the other person.

Blame is one of the gravest problems we face spiritually and emotionally. It keeps us more concerned about being "good" than about being honest. Learn to accept blame for what is truly yours and give up blaming for what is not another's fault.

So what can you do about your tendency to blame? First, learn to humbly listen to correction and restrain the urge to react in blame. Second, let blame signal you to see if you are afraid, feel judged, or are sad about a fault. Third, be more concerned about your own soul's state than that of your date's. Fourth, accept what is negative about your date and work with the realities instead of staying locked in protest, argument, and blame. Also, ask those you trust to let you know when you play the blame game. And, finally, be a forgiver—make mutual forgiveness a part of your dating relationships.

# Recommended Reading

"Don't Get Kidnapped," "Kiss False Hope Good-bye," and "Boundaries on Blame," chapters 12, 13, and 14 of *Boundaries in Dating*

# Session Eight

## Solving Dating Problems When You're Part of the Problem, Part 2

**3 MINUTES** **INTRODUCTION**

*1 minute* ### Welcome

> Call the group together and welcome the participants to Session 8, "Solving Dating Problems When You're Part of the Problem, Part 2."

*1 minute* ### Opening Prayer

Lord God, last time as we talked about dating problems, we saw that we can and do contribute to those problems. Today we're going to look at three more problems we may be contributing to in our dating relationships. Please, Lord, help us see ourselves with open eyes. And then remind us that, by your Holy Spirit, you are at work in us to change us. Use this session to grow us into the whole and healthy people you want us to be. We pray in Jesus' name. Amen.

*1 minute* ### Review and Overview

> Participant's Guide page 95.

Last time we met we talked about the dangers and the costs of adapting now and paying later and of too much, too fast. Both of those situations cause problems in dating relationships, problems which we ourselves contribute to.

# PLANNING NOTES

_____

_____

_____

_____

_____

_____

_____

_____

_____

_____

_____

*Session Eight*

## Solving Dating Problems When You're Part of the Problem, Part 2

### OVERVIEW

In this session you will

- Learn what it means to be kidnapped in a dating relationship and how to avoid it.

- Discover basic elements of safe dating so you can avoid being kidnapped.

- Look at the difference between false hope and merited hope, and when it is futile to hope a date will change.

- Define good blame and bad blame, consider whether you tend to blame rather than take responsibility, and learn how to put boundaries on the blame game.

95

Let's turn to page 95.

→ This week, we will first learn what it means to be kidnapped in a dating relationship and discover basic elements of safe dating so you can avoid being kidnapped. We will also look at the difference between false hope and merited hope and when it is futile to hope your date will change. Finally, we will define good blame and bad blame, consider whether we tend to blame rather than take responsibility, and learn how to put boundaries on the blame game.

Let's get started.

## 49 MINUTES DISCOVERY

## 6 minutes    *Video Segment 1: "Don't Get Kidnapped"*

The first problem we're going to look at is addressed in a video called "Don't Get Kidnapped." Let's watch it now.

> Remind the participants that key points from the video segment can be found on page 96 of the Participant's Guide if they would like to review them at a later time.

> View Video Segment 1: "Don't Get Kidnapped."

While it's easy to see what Debbie did wrong, it's not always so easy to see where *we're* not being wise or safe. But as Debbie learned, friends can give us some important ingredients that every dating relationship must have in order to be based in reality. Turn to page 97.

## 10 minutes    *On Your Own: Safe Dating*

> Participant's Guide page 97.

### Directions

On your own, please read the information and answer the questions found on pages 97–98. You will have 10 minutes to complete this exercise. Any questions?

> Let the participants know when there is 1 minute remaining. Call the group back together after 10 minutes.

## VIDEO SEGMENT
### *Don't Get Kidnapped*

- A relationship that gets rid of one's individual life and friends, time, and space is not a healthy relationship.
- Friends are an important space-giving freedom that will help you be healthier and more well-rounded. In addition, friends will notice if you are losing them to a dating relationship—and they'll let you know!
- Work out your dating relationship with the help of your friends. Spend time and energy with your dates, but then return to your community.
- One aspect of safe dating is to remain connected to your friends and support system. By doing so, you'll make sure that you are not vulnerable to what you cannot see on your own but would be able to see with the help of other people.
- Stay connected, stay safe, and stay wise.

## ON YOUR OWN
### *Safe Dating*

**DIRECTIONS**

On your own, please read the information and answer the questions found below. You will have 10 minutes to complete this exercise.

**Friends provide a feedback base to see reality.** The very state of being in love is a state of idealization, where the other person is not being viewed through the eyes of reality. We often can't see this idealization or the fact that we're becoming someone other than who we really are, but hopefully our friends can.

1. What chunks of reality about a person you've been in love with have you not seen? What helped you finally see them?

2. What role did friends play—or would you have liked them to play—in this realization?

**Friends provide a support base to deal with reality.** We do not deal with reality either because we do not see it or we see it and are unable or unwilling to deal with it. Many times we know there is something wrong, but we cannot find it in ourselves to break away or do the right thing. In these situations, friends often provide a support base to get us though.

3. When have you relied on friends to help you through some of life's hard times, perhaps even the end of a dating relationship?

4. How did your friends support you through this time?

**Friends help you stay connected to all parts of you.** A good relationship helps us to become more of who God made us to be, not less. If you are losing yourself in a relationship, friends can help you stay connected to the things you were connected with before you started dating.

5. When, if ever, have you lost parts of yourself in a dating relationship or perhaps even in a friendship? What parts did you lose?

**Friends help us stay grounded in spiritual values that make life work.** Our values are the architecture of life. They shape the way our life is going to be. When we begin to let our values slip, our life takes a direction that does not have a good end.

6. What values form the architecture of your life? List eight or ten.

7. In what ways might a dating relationship tempt you to compromise on these values? Thinking about this in advance may help you avoid some heartache.

## A FEW MORE THOUGHTS ON...
## HOPE IN YOUR DATING LIFE

Hope is one of the greatest _____ (1 Corinthians 13:13). The kind of hope God wants us to have is the kind that "does not _____" (Romans 5:5), the kind that is based on the love that God has for us. But the Bible speaks of another kind of hope as well. It is the hope that "makes the heart _____" (Proverbs 13:12), hope that is never realized, hope that does not give life. What is the role of hope in dating? When can we have hope that the person we are with is going to change?

To determine whether your hope is merited, consider two truths. First, it is _____ to continue to do the same thing expecting different results. Second, the best predictor of the _____, without some intervening variable, is the _____. These two truths can help you determine whether your current hope is merited. Be _____ with yourself.

Hope is a virtue. Hope should be based on _____. Hope can be distorted and lead to a broken heart. As you date, hope in _____, hope in his principles, hope in people of trustworthy _____, and hope in your own _____. Those are truly good reasons for hope. But don't throw hope away on things which have no reality behind them. That kind of hope makes the heart sick.

**2 minutes**

## A Few More Thoughts on ... Hope in Your Dating Life

> Participant's Guide page 99.

In dating, we're part of the problem when, because we don't build and maintain a strong support system of good friends, we let ourselves get kidnapped. We're also part of the problem when we cling to false hope. Please turn to page 99 and fill in the blanks as we go along.

➜ Hope is one of the greatest VIRTUES. The kind of hope God wants us to have is the kind that "does not DISAPPOINT," the kind that is based on the love that God has for us. But the Bible speaks of another kind of hope as well. It is the hope that "makes the heart SICK," hope that is never realized, hope that does not give life. What is the role of hope in dating? When can we have hope that the person we are with is going to change?

To determine whether your hope is merited, consider two truths. First, it is CRAZY to continue to do the same thing expecting different results. Second, the best predictor of the FUTURE, without some intervening variable, is the PAST. These two truths can help you determine whether your current hope is merited. Be HONEST with yourself.

Hope is a virtue. Hope should be based on REALITY. Hope can be distorted and lead to a broken heart. As you date, hope in GOD, hope in his principles, hope in people of trustworthy CHARACTER, and hope in your own GROWTH. Those are truly good reasons for hope. But don't throw hope away on things which have no reality behind them. That kind of hope makes the heart sick.

**15 minutes**

## Let's Talk: Good Hope or Bad Hope?

> Participant's Guide page 100.

So what is the role of hope in dating? Sometimes it's to hope for a date! But often it's the question of when to have hope that the person you are with is going to change. Please turn to page 100.

### Directions

1. I will be dividing you into four groups and assigning each group a scenario and accompanying questions.
2. Read through the scenario and discuss the questions, allowing everyone in the group to share. As before, italicized ques-

# PLANNING NOTES

_____

_____

_____

_____

_____

_____

_____

_____

_____

_____

_____

_____

_____

_____

_____

_____

_____

_____

_____

_____

_____

---

## A FEW MORE THOUGHTS ON...
## HOPE IN YOUR DATING LIFE

Hope is one of the greatest _____ (1 Corinthians 13:13). The kind of hope God wants us to have is the kind that "does not _____" (Romans 5:5), the kind that is based on the love that God has for us. But the Bible speaks of another kind of hope as well. It is the hope that "makes the heart _____" (Proverbs 13:12), hope that is never realized, hope that does not give life. What is the role of hope in dating? When can we have hope that the person we are with is going to change?

To determine whether your hope is merited, consider two truths. First, it is _____ to continue to do the same thing expecting different results. Second, the best predictor of the _____, without some intervening variable, is the _____. These two truths can help you determine whether your current hope is merited. Be _____ with yourself.

Hope is a virtue. Hope should be based on _____. Hope can be distorted and lead to a broken heart. As you date, hope in _____, hope in his principles, hope in people of trustworthy _____, and hope in your own _____. Those are truly good reasons for hope. But don't throw hope away on things which have no reality behind them. That kind of hope makes the heart sick.

---

## LET'S TALK

### *Good Hope or Bad Hope?*

**DIRECTIONS**

1. The leader will divide you into four groups and assign each group a scenario and accompanying questions.
2. Read through the scenario and discuss the questions, allowing everyone in the group to share. As before, italicized questions are part of your "Boundary Building" exercise, so disregard them for now.
3. The scenarios and each group's responses will be reviewed with the large group after the exercise is over.
4. You will have 5 minutes to complete this exercise.

**SCENARIO 1**

**The person you love treats you in a way that you cannot live with.**

Jayne was delightful. Her quick wit was part of her charm—at first. But at one point Scott realized that too often her sharpness seemed to bring laughs at his expense. He was frustrated that every time he tried to talk to her about it, she made a joke. He had even tried writing Jayne a letter to explain how her humor affected him and point to specific situations. Scott wasn't even sure she had taken the time to read the letter.

1. What could Jayne have done to give Scott hope that things were going to be different? What words and/or behaviors would have shown that she was taking ownership, that she wanted to be different, or that she had indeed heard what Scott was trying to tell her?

2. What advice would you give Scott?

tions are part of your "Boundary Building" exercise, so disregard them for now.

3. We will review the scenarios and each group's responses with the large group after the exercise is over.

4. You will have 5 minutes to complete this exercise. Any questions?

> Let the participants know when there is 1 minute remaining. Call the group together after 5 minutes.

Okay, let's review the first scenario. The person Scott loved treated him in a way he couldn't live with. Who from that group would be willing to read the scenario and share with us what their group came up with?

> Possible answers could include: apologizing and asking forgiveness; talking to Scott about the times she had hurt him so she could learn to change. Advice may include: shoot some biting humor Jayne's way, set boundaries ("I'll leave the next time you make a joke at my expense in public"), or call off the relationship.

Those were some good comments. Dr. Cloud and Dr. Townsend think that the best hope is to be involved in God's growth process yourself and to pursue good character qualities. The more you are a person of the light, the more you will be able to recognize people who are worth hoping for.

Let's move on to the second scenario. The second group looked at a situation where a person says that she "likes" or "loves" her partner but is not "in love" with him and wants more time to see where the relationship is going. Who would be willing to read that scenario and summarize their group's questions?

> Possible feedback about Kelli could include: "She may be afraid of being rejected or hurt if she really lets herself get closer to Luke"; "She may not be being honest with Luke"; and "If she just came out of a bad relationship, she may just need time." Advice to Luke may include: "Don't waste your time"; "There are other fish in the sea"; "Don't trust her. She's just leading you on"; or "Give her time if you think she's worth the wait."

Boundaries have to do with taking responsibility for reality. You know where the other person stands, and now it is your choice—take control of yourself and do what you think is best. But if one of the parties in the relationship has been acting like more than a friend and then tells the other person that you are just friends, Dr. Townsend and Dr. Cloud advise you to get moving. Let's move on to our third scenario.

The third group considered what to do when a dating partner won't commit to the relationship's future. Who would be willing to read

## LET'S TALK

### *Good Hope or Bad Hope?*

**DIRECTIONS**

1. The leader will divide you into four groups and assign each group a scenario and accompanying questions.

2. Read through the scenario and discuss the questions, allowing everyone in the group to share. As before, italicized questions are part of your "Boundary Building" exercise, so disregard them for now.

3. The scenarios and each group's responses will be reviewed with the large group after the exercise is over.

4. You will have 5 minutes to complete this exercise.

**SCENARIO 1**

**The person you love treats you in a way that you cannot live with.**

Jayne was delightful. Her quick wit was part of her charm—at first. But at one point Scott realized that too often her sharpness seemed to bring laughs at his expense. He was frustrated that every time he tried to talk to her about it, she made a joke. He had even tried writing Jayne a letter to explain how her humor affected him and point to specific situations. Scott wasn't even sure she had taken the time to read the letter.

1. What could Jayne have done to give Scott hope that things were going to be different? What words and/or behaviors would have shown that she was taking ownership, that she wanted to be different, or that she had indeed heard what Scott was trying to tell her?

2. What advice would you give Scott?

3. *If the person you love treats you in a way that you cannot live with, how are you dealing with it? Is your hope merited? What reason has he or she given you to hope that things are going to be different? Is that reason sustainable?*

4. Are you seeing evidence of true change and growth? Is there more ownership, a growth path, hunger for change, involvement in some system of change, repentance, or other fruits of a change of direction? Is there self-motivation for change, or is it all coming from you?

**SCENARIO 2**

**A person you are dating says he or she "likes you" or "loves you" but is not "in love with you" and wants more time to see where the relationship is going.**

Luke knew right away that there was something different about Kelli. She had a way of bringing out the best in him. She clearly seemed to enjoy being with him, she laughed at his jokes, she listened carefully as he described the challenges of his teaching day, and she readily helped him grade papers (what a lame excuse to be together, but she offered!). He knew she readily canceled plans with her girlfriends when he called at the last minute. All of these signs—and more—were very encouraging. But still Kelli insisted that she loved Luke but wasn't "in love" with him.

1. What might be behind Kelli's word game? Imagine what she might be feeling or fearing.

2. Which of the following pieces of advice would you give Luke? Why?
   — Tell Kelli that you have enjoyed your time together, but you are developing more feelings than she is, so you do not see any reason in going forward if it is not mutual. Then end the dating relationship.

   — End the relationship and don't go back for any reason.

   — Tell Kelli that you are willing to continue if she feels like more time is going to help.

   — Continue with your eyes wide open.

3. *If Luke's situation is a lot like your current situation, have you tried to take the relationship to a different level from the "just friends" status? What did you do and how were your efforts received?*

4. If you have let your feelings be known, but nothing seems to have changed, you (like Luke) could do one of the following. Which will you choose and why?
   *—Tell your date that you have enjoyed your time together, but you are developing more feelings than he or she is, so you*

   *do not see any reason in going forward if it is not mutual. Then end the dating relationship.*

   — End the relationship and don't go back for any reason.

   — Tell your date that you are willing to continue if he or she feels like more time is going to help.

   — Continue with your eyes wide open.

**SCENARIO 3**

**Your dating partner won't commit to the relationship's future.**

Sherry knew Tim loved her. Why else would he spend most of his free time with her? Why else would he take her on such great getaways and regularly surprise her with such expensive gifts? And why else would he have been so helpful these last three months since her mom broke her hip and that whole nursing home nightmare had begun? So why, Sherry wondered, wouldn't Tim commit to the relationship's future? Their lives certainly seemed to be getting more and more entwined, but Tim made it clear he didn't want to talk about the "M" word!

1. Why might Tim be reluctant to commit to his future with Sherry?

through the third scenario and give us some feedback on that group's responses?

> Possible answers to questions about Tim's reluctance could include: "He may have just gotten out of a bad situation"; "He may not have any good models for marriage"; "He may just not be the marrying type"; or "He's a chicken." Participants may advise Sherry to pull the plug on the relationship; to give him a time frame or at least have a time frame in her mind about when time is up; or to keep praying and waiting.

Those are some great insights. Time does run out and you can reach a point in a relationship where there is no reason to hope that more time is going to solve anything. In that case, you need to set a limit and stick to it. When you reach that limit, give up hope and move on with your life.

Finally, our fourth scenario. The fourth group talked about what happens when you want a friend to like you in a different way, but it's not happening. Who would be willing to read that scenario and go over that group's answers and advice?

> Participants might advise Katie to be open and honest about what she's feeling, to find ways to spend more time with Garrett, or to encourage conversations to go deeper than they have before. Possible risks Katie would be taking in doing these things include embarrassment, rejection, and the loss of a friendship—and only she can decide if the possible gain is worth the risk.

Thanks for that feedback. Remember: Just hoping that a person's feelings are going to change for no good reason other than you want them to would be foolish.

## 6 minutes    *Video Segment 2: "Boundaries on Blame"*

So far today we've looked at the problems that arise when we let ourselves get kidnapped and when we cling to false hope that the person we're dating will change. We'll look at one more problem we can cause, and that's the issue of blaming. Let's hear what Dr. Cloud and Dr. Townsend have to say about blame.

> Remind the participants that key points from the video can be found on page 106 of the Participant's Guide if they would like to review them at a later time.

> View Video Segment 2: "Boundaries on Blame."

*do not see any reason in going forward if it is not mutual. Then end the dating relationship.*

— End the relationship and don't go back for any reason.

— Tell your date that you are willing to continue if he or she feels like more time is going to help.

— Continue with your eyes wide open.

**SCENARIO 3**

**Your dating partner won't commit to the relationship's future.**

Sherry knew Tim loved her. Why else would he spend most of his free time with her? Why else would he take her on such great getaways and regularly surprise her with such expensive gifts? And why else would he have been so helpful these last three months since her mom broke her hip and that whole nursing home nightmare had begun? So why, Sherry wondered, wouldn't Tim commit to the relationship's future? Their lives certainly seemed to be getting more and more entwined, but Tim made it clear he didn't want to talk about the "M" word!

1. Why might Tim be reluctant to commit to his future with Sherry?

2. What advice would you give Sherry? Why?

3. *If you are currently facing this situation, why might your partner be reluctant? Is he certain about you but doubtful about the timing? Or is he dealing with commitment phobia or commitment allergy? Support your answer with specifics— and get a friend's perspective too.*

4. Is the handwriting on the wall? Is it time to pull the plug? What will you do to let your support system do its job for you?

**SCENARIO 4**

**You want a friend to like you in a different way, but it is not happening.**

Katie had known Garrett for a long time and in a variety of settings, and the more she saw of him, the more she was attracted to him. He'd always been a great friend, helping her move into her new apartment, calling her when there was another opening on the church's coed softball team, and always willing to grab the latest Tom Hanks movie with her. And a few months ago when Garrett spent that Saturday with her and her three young and less-than-well-behaved nephews, she knew she was falling in love. He was great with kids! But, despite Katie's wish for their friendship to become something more, nothing had happened.

1. What advice would you give Katie? What could she do or say that might spark a change?

2. What risk does Katie take if she chooses to do something different in the relationship in hopes of bringing about a change? How could she decide if the possible gain is worth the risk?

3. *If you currently find yourself in this situation, what statement (openness and honesty about what you're thinking and feeling? discussing what dating each other would be like?) or action (greater knowledge of each other? spending more time together?) might be an "intervening variable" that sparks a change?*

4. Are you doing something different in the relationship that could bring about change? Or are you continuing to do the same things expecting different results? If you have not tried something different, there may be some hope if you change.

**VIDEO SEGMENT**

***Boundaries on Blame***

- We're part of a dating problem when we don't put boundaries on blame.
- Blaming is ascribing responsibility to someone for a fault. When we accuse another of a problem, we are blaming.
- Blame is not bad in and of itself; it has a good function. Blame separates out who is truly responsible for what in a problem, so that we are able to know how to solve it. Blame helps differentiate between what is our fault and what is another's.
- The blame that kills a good dating relationship is when one person sees herself as blameless and attributes almost all of the problems in the relationship to the other person.
- Blame can be one of the gravest problems we face spiritually and emotionally. It keeps us more concerned about being "good" than about being honest.
- Learn to humbly listen to correction and restrain the urge to react in blame. Let blame signal you to see if you are afraid, feel judged, or are sad about a fault. Be more concerned about your own soul's state than that of your date's. Also, ask those you trust to let you know when you play the blame game.
- Accept what is negative about your date and work with the realities instead of staying locked in protest, argument, and blame.
- Be a forgiver—make mutual forgiveness a part of your dating relationships.

Blame can be a good thing or a bad thing. Blame can separate out who is truly responsible for what in a problem so that we are able to know how to solve it. But blame can also do great damage. We're going to look at "the blame game" and then we'll start considering how to cure blame. Please turn to page 107.

## *10 minutes*     *A Few More Thoughts on . . . Blame*

> Participant's Guide page 107.

### The Blame Game

Let's first spend some time talking about the blame game and how it impacts dating relationships.

➜ Blaming has the power to negate the growth of INTIMACY in a dating relationship.

When someone feels continually blamed by his date, he is in conflict between his desire to open up and his impulse to withdraw protectively.

➜ You don't even have to verbally blame the other person to ruin the relationship. Blaming can be done in your ATTITUDE, without your speaking a word.

Can anyone give me an instance in which blame was communicated even though words were unspoken?

> Solicit answers from the group. Possible answers may include silence, coldness, distance, and sarcasm.

➜ Ultimately, blame is its own and only REWARD.

There is a very sick satisfaction that comes in pointing the finger of judgment at another. Blaming provides us with the delusion that we are better than we are and that our biggest problems in life are the sins of other people.

How does this wrong perspective on ourselves block our relationship with God and with other people?

> Solicit answers from the group. Possible answers may include: "Our lack of honesty distances us from God and others" or "Our arrogant sense that we are better than we are can keep people from wanting to get to know us."

# PLANNING NOTES

_____

_____

_____

_____

_____

_____

_____

_____

_____

_____

_____

_____

_____

_____

_____

_____

_____

_____

_____

_____

_____

_____

_____

_____

---

## VIDEO SEGMENT
### *Boundaries on Blame*

- We're part of a dating problem when we don't put boundaries on blame.

- Blaming is ascribing responsibility to someone for a fault. When we accuse another of a problem, we are blaming.

- Blame is not bad in and of itself; it has a good function. Blame separates out who is truly responsible for what in a problem, so that we are able to know how to solve it. Blame helps differentiate between what is our fault and what is another's.

- The blame that kills a good dating relationship is when one person sees herself as blameless and attributes almost all of the problems in the relationship to the other person.

- Blame can be one of the gravest problems we face spiritually and emotionally. It keeps us more concerned about being "good" than about being honest.

- Learn to humbly listen to correction and restrain the urge to react in blame. Let blame signal you to see if you are afraid, feel judged, or are sad about a fault. Be more concerned about your own soul's state than that of your date's. Also, ask those you trust to let you know when you play the blame game.

- Accept what is negative about your date and work with the realities instead of staying locked in protest, argument, and blame.

- Be a forgiver—make mutual forgiveness a part of your dating relationships.

---

## A FEW MORE THOUGHTS ON ...
## BLAME
### *The Blame Game*

- Blaming has the power to negate the growth of _____ in a dating relationship.

- You don't even have to verbally blame the other person to ruin the relationship. Blaming can be done in your _____, without your speaking a word.

- Ultimately, blame is its own and only _____.

- Finally, blame can kill a dating relationship when the injured person takes on an attitude of _____ to her offender.

### *Five Guidelines for Curing Blame*

1. Become _____. The most important solution is to actively observe your own soul for faults and weaknesses.

2. Relate to both the _____ and _____ of your date. It is hard to maintain a blaming stance if you keep the good parts of your date in mind as much as you do the bad parts.

3. Set _____ instead of _____. Many times people blame because it is the only way they can protest what the other person is doing.

4. _____. Another reason people continually blame is that they have difficulty forgiving their date. Forgiveness is canceling a debt that someone owes.

5. _____. While forgiveness is objective in nature, grief is its emotional component. When we cancel a debt, we are letting go of the right to demand revenge. That letting go brings loss and a feeling of sadness.

→ Finally, blame can kill a dating relationship when the injured person takes on an attitude of MORAL SUPERIORITY to her offender.

Why is living in the reality that we are all sinners actually less work than living in a fantasy land of moral superiority? How can assuming a morally superior position work against everything a person wants in life, especially in relationships?

Solicit answers from the group. Possible answers to the first question may include: "We can be honest about our mistakes"; "We don't have to pretend who we are—and pretending takes a lot of work"; and, to the second question, "A morally superior position sure doesn't attract people, so that's no way to get into a good relationship."

Okay. Now let's talk a bit about some guidelines for curing blame.

## Five Guidelines for Curing Blame

→ First, become SELF-SCRUTINIZING. The most important solution is to actively observe your own soul for faults and weaknesses.

Second, relate to both the GOOD and BAD of your date. It is hard to maintain a blaming stance if you keep the good parts of your date in mind as much as you do the bad parts.

Third, set BOUNDARIES instead of BLAMING. Many times people blame because it is the only way they can protest what the other person is doing.

It is much more helpful to confront your date in love, let him know what you will not tolerate, and set limits if the behavior continues.

Fourth, FORGIVE. Another reason people continually blame is that they have difficulty forgiving their date. Forgiveness is canceling a debt that someone owes.

And, finally, GRIEVE. While forgiveness is objective in nature, grief is its emotional component. When we cancel a debt, we are letting go of the right to demand revenge. That letting go brings loss and a feeling of sadness.

These five steps for curing blame involve some work, but they will effectively set limits on the negative power of blame in your relationship.

# PLANNING NOTES

---

## A FEW MORE THOUGHTS ON . . . BLAME

### The Blame Game

- Blaming has the power to negate the growth of _____ in a dating relationship.

- You don't even have to verbally blame the other person to ruin the relationship. Blaming can be done in your _____, without your speaking a word.

- Ultimately, blame is its own and only _____.

- Finally, blame can kill a dating relationship when the injured person takes on an attitude of _____ to her offender.

### Five Guidelines for Curing Blame

1. Become _____. The most important solution is to actively observe your own soul for faults and weaknesses.

2. Relate to both the _____ and _____ of your date. It is hard to maintain a blaming stance if you keep the good parts of your date in mind as much as you do the bad parts.

3. Set _____ instead of _____. Many times people blame because it is the only way they can protest what the other person is doing.

4. _____. Another reason people continually blame is that they have difficulty forgiving their date. Forgiveness is canceling a debt that someone owes.

5. _____. While forgiveness is objective in nature, grief is its emotional component. When we cancel a debt, we are letting go of the right to demand revenge. That letting go brings loss and a feeling of sadness.

## 3 MINUTES    SUMMARY

We've covered a lot of humbling territory in this session. We've looked at how we are part of the problem in a dating relationship when we let ourselves get kidnapped, when we cling to false hope, and when we don't put boundaries on blame. But we've also looked at how we can solve these three problems. Staying in community as we date, for instance, can help us avoid being kidnapped. We can and need to be honest with ourselves as we consider whether it is wise to have hope for a relationship. And we need to stop playing the blame game.

This week, in your "Boundary Building" exercise, keep addressing the problem of blame by working on the "Curing Blame" exercise on pages 108–10. Also, spend some time in prayer asking God to show you both where you are contributing to dating problems and what he would have you do about that.

## *2 minutes*    *Closing Prayer*

Lord God, you've shown us several ways we can contribute to problems in dating. Help us to avoid the problem of being kidnapped by staying in touch with friends even as we date. And help us hear your voice through what our friends have to say about things we cannot see. And help us always to heed your will and live life your way in every aspect of our life, including our dating.

We also ask, Lord, that you help us avoid the problem of clinging to false hope. Please make us people who hope in you, who stand on your sound principles of growth, and who keep working with you on our own growth. Keep us rooted in reality and trusting you when we turn to you for guidance as to whether or not we should have hope about a relationship.

Third, Lord, help us avoid the blame game. We know that blame can kill a dating relationship or friendship, but we also know it's a much easier option. So in our relationships please help us be more concerned about being honest than "good," more concerned about our own sinfulness than our date's or our friend's. Help us also to humbly listen to correction and grow from it and to forgive as you have forgiven us.

Finally, thank you that when you show us where we're blowing it or where we've been injured and need healing, you don't leave us alone and hopeless. Thank you that your Spirit is active in making us more the people you want us to be. In Jesus' name. Amen.

# PLANNING NOTES

_____

_____

_____

_____

_____

_____

_____

_____

_____

_____

_____

---

## ON YOUR OWN
### *Curing Blame*

**DIRECTIONS**

As part of your "Boundary Building" exercise this week, consider the "Five Guidelines for Curing Blame" and work through the following questions.

1. Which of your own faults and weaknesses—especially those that greatly impact your friendships and dating relationships—are you very much aware of?

2. What will you do to become aware of your faults if, up to this point, you have chosen to remain blind to them? Whom, for instance, will you trust to speak the truth in love to you?

3. Explore why it is difficult for you to look at your faults. Do you feel easily condemned or "bad"? Do you feel all alone when your faults are evident? Have you not had much experience in taking criticism and feeling loved? Begin to work on these issues.

4. Why is relating to both the good and bad of your date not denial—and why is chronic blaming closer to denial?

5. When, if ever, have you been very aware of a date or a friend accepting the bad as well as the good in you? How did you know about that person's awareness of your bad? How does being accepted despite your bad strengthen a relationship?

---

6. Think about a dating relationship or friendship where you were the "blamee." What boundaries could the blamer have been working on setting instead of merely blaming you?

7. When, if ever, have you found it easier to blame instead of set boundaries? Be specific about the dynamics of the friendship or dating relationship.

8. Blaming never really solves the problem you have. Limits often do, and thus eliminate the need for blaming in the first place. When, if ever, have you experienced or seen limits solve a problem in a dating relationship or friendship? Be specific about the work of setting boundaries and how those boundaries were received.

9. When, if ever, have you felt blamed rather than forgiven? What impact did that have on the relationship? And when, if ever, have you chosen to blame rather than to forgive? Why did you make that choice, and what were the results of your decision?

10. Our advice is to set limits on what can change, and to deal with and forgive what will not. In what current relationship, dating or otherwise, do you have an opportunity to forgive? Make it a topic of prayer and action.

11. While forgiveness is objective in nature, grief is its emotional component. When we cancel a debt, we are letting go of the right to demand revenge. That letting go brings loss and a feeling of sadness. When, if ever, have you lost the battle for a person to change, to see things your way, or to understand just how much she hurt you? What did you do with your anger at that

---

loss—hold on to it or let go of it and grieve? What impact did your choice have on the relationship?

12. Every day God lets go and feels sad about how we choose to conduct our lives (Matthew 23:37). What does this truth help you see about yourself and about how God would have you treat other people?

## Boundary Building

This week spend some time answering the questions in "Safe Dating," "Good Hope or Bad Hope?" and "Curing Blame." You might also spend some time in prayer asking God to show you both where you are contributing to any current dating problems and what he would have you do about that.

## Suggested Reading

For more thoughts on this session's topics, read chapters 12, 13, and 14 in *Boundaries in Dating*: "Don't Get Kidnapped," "Kiss False Hope Good-bye," and "Boundaries on Blame." For a more thorough self-evaluation, look at chapters 12, 13, and 14 in the *Boundaries in Dating Workbook*.

# *Session Nine*

# Solving Dating Problems When Your Date Is the Problem

## BEFORE YOU LEAD

### *Key Points*

- Respect is the ability to value another's experience. Empathy is the ability to feel another's experience, especially a painful one. Any relationship needs both. When respect is present, the other person feels that he can be free to be who he is.

- A disrespectful relationship has to do, ultimately, with character. Disrespect can be caused by selfishness, control, lack of understanding, and other things. Address early in the relationship any disrespect you notice. Also, see if you are making it easier to be disrespected by putting yourself in a position of inferiority and letting yourself be treated accordingly.

- In relationships, you get what you tolerate, so set your limits early on. Make them clear. Enforce them and stick to them.

- Boundaries should be woven into the fabric of your life and relationships as something you do and say daily. Setting limits is simply being honest about what you allow and don't allow. Make honesty, responsibility, respect, and freedom a required part of all aspects of your relationship.

- See boundaries as tools for diagnosing the character of your date and of the relationship. Basically, think about boundaries as preserving the relationship, not ending it.

- When you set boundaries, you are allowing pain—the pain of consequences for their actions—to touch someone important to you.

- Everyone needs to be involved in the process of spiritual growth. This means being in a process in which a person brings his struggles, weaknesses, and vulnerabilities to God and some safe people on an ongoing basis. As he confesses his sins and failings, he receives forgiveness, comfort, and truth to work through his issues over time, and God grows him up.

# *Synopsis*

Having looked at how to solve several dating problems that arise when we're part of the problem, in this session we'll look at how to solve three dating problems that arise when our *date* is the problem.

**Address disrespect.** Respect is the ability to value another's experience. When respect is present, the other person feels he can be free to be who he is. He can be honest and still feel connected and safe. He doesn't worry that he will be attacked, humiliated, or treated poorly.

A disrespectful relationship has ultimately to do with character. Disrespect can be caused by selfishness, control, lack of understanding, and other things. Keep in mind that, if someone is genuinely trying to change his disrespectful ways, it is not disrespectful to fail. It is, however, disrespectful to continually fail in an area that hurts another and not take steps to resolve the failure.

So respect and esteem your date's thoughts, feelings, and choices—and require that sort of treatment from him. Address early in the relationship any disrespect you notice. Start from a position of vulnerability and state your desire for the relationship to be better.

**Set limits.** In relationships, you get what you tolerate, so set your limits early on. Make them clear. Enforce them and stick to them. Setting the tone early in how you expect to be treated will weed out the selfish people, discipline the sloppy ones, and show your date that you have self-respect and will not tolerate being treated poorly.

The following should not be tolerated for very long: being inconsiderate regarding time or commitments; not following through on promises or commitments; disrespectful comments that are degrading or otherwise hurtful; pushing for physical relationship past where you allow; unfair or irresponsible financial dealings; critical attitudes; other consistent ways of hurting your feelings that are clearly his or her fault and not your own sensitivities; or controlling behavior. The truth of saying what bothers you is the best policy, but say it in love without sinning yourself.

**Respond in a healthy way.** Though no one has the power to fix anyone else, you do have the power to respond in healthy ways to your date when problems arise.

First of all, realize that some conflict is normal. Problems, including boundary conflicts, are a normal part of relationships. So give up the demand that your relationship be conflict-free, get over it, and go to the next step.

That step is to require boundaries in your relationship. Be honest about what you allow and don't allow. If that sounds scary, deal with your fear of setting limits. See boundaries as tools for diagnosing the character of your date and of the relationship. Basically, think about boundaries as preserving the relationship, not ending it.

Then, when you set boundaries, remember that you are allowing pain—the pain of consequences for their actions—to touch someone important to you. The conflict of wanting closeness yet having to take a righteous stance with a boundaryless person can take its toll. We've identified seven things to have in place as you go through the boundary-setting process: stay connected to good people; avoid reactive friends; expect negative reactions; empathize with the struggle; be patient; question your date's motives; and provide a way back to normality.

Finally, as you date, look for someone involved in spiritual growth, someone who brings his struggles, weaknesses, and vulnerabilities to God and some safe people on an ongoing basis. As he confesses his sins and failings, he receives forgiveness, comfort, and truth to work through his issues over time, and God grows him up. Find someone who loves God and who you can grow with. Then enjoy the journey together!

## Recommended Reading

"Say No to Disrespect," "Nip It in the Bud," and "Set Up a Detention Hall," chapters 15, 16, and 18 of *Boundaries in Dating*

# Session Nine

## Solving Dating Problems When Your Date Is the Problem

### 3 MINUTES    INTRODUCTION

**1 minute**    ### Welcome

> Call the group together and welcome the participants to Session 9, "Solving Dating Problems: When Your Date Is Part of the Problem."

**1 minute**    ### Opening Prayer

Lord God, we've spent two humbling sessions looking at how we contribute to dating problems and what to do to avoid those problems. Please keep us humble as, in this session, we look at what to do when our date is the problem. Teach us not only what to do if we're in this situation, but also show us where we may be causing this exact kind of dating problem in someone else's life. We pray in Jesus' name. Amen.

**1 minute**    ### Review and Overview

> Participant's Guide page 111.

We've spent a couple sessions looking at problems that we may be causing, or at least contributing to, in our dating. We looked at adapting to our date rather than being ourselves; at moving too fast in a relationship; at letting ourselves get kidnapped by our date; at holding on

144

# PLANNING NOTES

_____

_____

_____

_____

_____

_____

_____

_____

_____

_____

_____

_____

*Session Nine*

## Solving Dating Problems When Your Date Is the Problem

### OVERVIEW

In this session you will

- Learn how to say no to your date's disrespect.

- Recognize the importance of setting limits on what behaviors you'll tolerate and not tolerate.

- Use boundaries as tools for both diagnosing the character of your relationship and for laying down consequences so that the relationship can improve.

- Acknowledge that everyone needs to be involved in the process of spiritual growth.

111

_____

_____

_____

_____

_____

_____

_____

_____

_____

_____

_____

_____

_____

_____

to false hope; and at playing the blame game rather than taking appropriate responsibility.

Let's turn to page 111.

→ Today we're going to look at ways in which our date is part of the problem. We'll talk about saying no to our date's disrespect; setting limits on what behaviors we'll tolerate and not tolerate; and using boundaries both to diagnose the character of your relationship and to lay down consequences so that the relationship can improve. Before we close, we'll also talk about how everyone needs to be involved in the process of spiritual growth.

## 47 MINUTES DISCOVERY

Let's take a look at the first way our date can be part of the problem: disrespect.

### 6 minutes

## *Video Segment 1: "Say No to Disrespect"*

> Remind the participants that key points from the video segment can be found on page 112 of the Participant's Guide if they would like to review them at a later time.

> View Video Segment 1: "Say No to Disrespect."

As we've just heard, respect is not worship. Instead, it has more to do with Jesus' Golden Rule (Matthew 7:12). What do you do or not do to show your respect for a friend or a date?

> Solicit answers from the group. Possible answers are: common courtesy; following through when you say you'll do something; avoiding sarcasm; encouraging; complimenting; speaking the truth in love; being honest.

What behaviors, if any, have made you feel disrespected by a date? More specifically, when have you felt dominated, manipulated, violated, minimized, or blamed?

> Solicit answers from the group. Possible answers are: "When my wishes have been ignored"; "When my date doesn't listen to me"; "When we always do what my date wants"; or "When my date is late and doesn't apologize."

# PLANNING NOTES

_____

_____

_____

_____

_____

_____

_____

_____

_____

_____

_____

_____

_____

_____

_____

_____

_____

_____

_____

_____

_____

_____

_____

_____

---

*Session Nine*

## Solving Dating Problems When Your Date Is the Problem

### OVERVIEW

In this session you will

- Learn how to say no to your date's disrespect.
- Recognize the importance of setting limits on what behaviors you'll tolerate and not tolerate.
- Use boundaries as tools for both diagnosing the character of your relationship and for laying down consequences so that the relationship can improve.
- Acknowledge that everyone needs to be involved in the process of spiritual growth.

111

---

112     *Boundaries in Dating Paticipant's Guide*

### VIDEO SEGMENT
#### *Say No to Disrespect*

- Respect is the ability to value another's experience. Empathy is the ability to feel another's experience, especially a painful one. Any relationship needs both. You may not be able to actually empathize with someone, but you can always take a position of respect for them.
- Disrespect is a serious obstacle to closeness, intimacy, and a couple's chances for marital success. When respect is present, the other person feels that he can be free to be who he is.
- A disrespectful relationship has to do, ultimately, with character. Disrespect can be caused by selfishness, control, lack of understanding, and other things.
- Respect and esteem your date's thoughts, feelings, and choices—and require that sort of treatment from him. Address early in the relationship any disrespect you notice.
- Don't fight fire with fire. Start with vulnerability and state your desire for the relationship to be better.
- See if you are making it easier to be disrespected by putting yourself in a position of inferiority in the relationship and letting yourself be treated as such.
- Make a distinction between differences and disrespect. You can disagree and even get angry with each other *respectfully*.

Ending the relationship immediately, putting up with disrespect, retaliating with disrespect, or complaining about being treated disrespectfully but not enforcing consequences will not cure disrespect. Let's look at what actions *can* go a long way toward resolving a disrespectful dating relationship. Please turn to page 113.

**15 minutes**

## Let's Talk: "What Cures Disrespect"

> Participant's Guide page 113.

### Directions

1. I will be dividing you into seven groups and assigning each group one cure for disrespect from page 113–14.
2. Each group will have about 5 minutes to plan and practice a one- to two-minute role-play based on their assigned "cure." After I call the group back together, each small group will present their scene to the rest of the class.
3. The "For personal reflection" question is part of this week's "Boundary Building" exercise, so please disregard it for now. Any questions?

> Divide the group into seven small groups and assign each a cure from pages 113–114 of the Participant's Guide. Let the participants know when there is 1 minute remaining. Call the group back together after 5 minutes. Going through the list of cures, have each group present their role-play. Note: in the interests of time, make sure to keep the role-plays only 1 to 2 minutes long.

In curing disrespect, change what you need to change, but require that your date treat you respectfully. When you do this, you either get more respect from those who have it to give, or you get left by those who don't have it. Both results are good ones.

Now let's look at another problem your date may be causing. Please turn to page 116.

**5 minutes**

## A Few More Thoughts on ... Getting What You Tolerate

> Participant's Guide page 116.

Consider the following relationship. During their relationship, Todd was being inconsiderate. He would just not show up for things

## LET'S TALK

### *What Cures Disrespect*

**DIRECTIONS**

1. The leader will be dividing you into seven groups and assigning each group one cure for disrespect listed below.

2. Each group will have about 5 minutes to plan and practice a one- to two-minute role-play based on their assigned "cure." After the group is called back together, each small group will present their scene to the rest of the class.

3. The "For personal reflection" question is part of this week's "Boundary Building" exercise, so please disregard it for now.

**7 CURES FOR DISRESPECT**

1. **Deal with it right away.** What conversation might happen on the second or third date? Be sure to speak the truth in love.

2. **Get to know your date in the context of other relationships.** What realization might you have after seeing your date interact with other people? Are you the guilty party whose demands are too high? Is your date treating you differently than he treats others? In role-playing, share with the disrespectful date your insights about the difference in his or her behavior in the context of other relationships.

3. **Say no to your date's preference.** This isn't as easy as it may sound. Show how the disrespecter will try to change your no to yes.

4. **Address the disrespect problem.** See if the disrespect is rooted in ignorance by telling the disrespecter that you feel controlled, dismissed, or unheard. Have the disrespecter respond with rationalization, denial, blame, or an apology and a real desire to change.

5. **Clarify.** Address what bothers you about the disrespectful behavior, how you feel when you are disrespected, how you would like to be treated, and what you will do if things do not change. Show both an effective way of saying these things and the disrespecter's response (rationalization, denial, blame, or an apology and a real desire to change.)

6. **Bring others in.** Get support, feedback, and reality testing from safe friends. Role-play a conversation between a person who is being disrespected and a safe friend who can offer support and reality testing.

7. **Own your own part.** Role-play a person being disrespected talking to a safe friend and recognizing the guilt of not saying anything, which can imply consent; of treating the disrespect lightly; of vacillating between doing nothing and being enraged; or of making it all his fault and problem instead of his date's. Have the safe friend offer some helpful input.

### *For Personal Reflection*

Think about disrespect from the other perspective. What disrespectful behaviors, if any, might you be guilty of in a dating relationship (past or present) or a friendship? The following list of actions that show respect might help you see where you may fall short.

- You hear and value your date's opinion.
- You validate differences and disagreements.
- You esteem your date's choices, even the wrong ones.
- You consider your date's feelings.
- You confront the other person respectfully, you do not talk down to them or baby them.

## A FEW MORE THOUGHTS ON. . . GETTING WHAT YOU TOLERATE

Patience and the ability to overlook some offenses are wonderful qualities (Proverbs 19:11), but overlooking certain negative character patterns long-term can lead to a real problem. Some weeds are worth confronting. The following should not be tolerated for very long:

- Being inconsiderate regarding _____ or commitments
- Not following through on _____ or commitments
- _____ comments that are degrading or otherwise hurtful
- Pushing for _____ relationship past where you allow
- Unfair or irresponsible _____ dealings
- _____ attitudes
- Other consistent ways of _____ your feelings that are clearly his or her fault and not your own sensitivities
- _____ behavior

they had planned. Even when Mary asked him to let her know if something came up, he never would. She tried to tell him a few times how much his behavior bothered her, but he really wasn't listening. He seemed to do pretty much what he wanted to do, and Mary was supposed to be fine with it.

The problem was made worse because Mary never set any boundaries with Todd. She never told him, for instance, that if he were not on time or did not keep the date, he could forget getting together that night. Doing that seemed mean to her. So instead of being "mean," Mary allowed Todd to take advantage of her niceness and to not be responsible in the relationship. Finally, Mary couldn't tolerate Todd's behavior anymore and called things off—much to Todd's surprise!

Have you ever found yourself in a situation like this? A better way of dealing with dating behavior is to set your limits early on. Make them clear. Enforce them and stick to them. In short, nip the problem in the bud and do not allow it to grow in the garden of your relationships. Setting the tone early in how you expect to be treated will weed out the selfish people, discipline the sloppy ones, and show your date that you have self-respect and will not tolerate being treated poorly.

→ Patience and the ability to overlook some offenses are wonderful qualities (Proverbs 19:11), but overlooking certain negative character patterns long-term can lead to a real problem. Some weeds are worth confronting. The following should not be tolerated for very long:

- Being inconsiderate regarding TIME or commitments
- Not following through on PROMISES or commitments
- DISRESPECTFUL comments that are degrading or otherwise hurtful
- Pushing for PHYSICAL relationship past where you allow
- Unfair or irresponsible FINANCIAL dealings
- CRITICAL attitudes
- Other consistent ways of HURTING your feelings that are clearly his or her fault and not your own sensitivities
- CONTROLLING behavior

Keep in mind that the best accounts are short ones (Ephesians 4:25–27). Tell the person that you won't tolerate certain things and that, if they continue, he or she cannot see you until they learn how to not act that way. The truth of saying what bothers you is the best policy. But say it in love without sinning yourself.

As part of this week's "Boundary Building," you'll think more personally about these nipping-it-in-the-bud principles. Right now we're going to look at one more dating problem that your date may be contributing to.

# PLANNING NOTES

_____

_____

_____

_____

_____

_____

_____

_____

_____

_____

_____

_____

---

### A FEW MORE THOUGHTS ON...
### GETTING WHAT YOU TOLERATE

Patience and the ability to overlook some offenses are wonderful qualities (Proverbs 19:11), but overlooking certain negative character patterns long-term can lead to a real problem. Some weeds are worth confronting. The following should not be tolerated for very long:

- Being inconsiderate regarding _____ or commitments

- Not following through on _____ or commitments

- _____ comments that are degrading or otherwise hurtful

- Pushing for _____ relationship past where you allow

- Unfair or irresponsible _____ dealings

- _____ attitudes

- Other consistent ways of _____ your feelings that are clearly his or her fault and not your own sensitivities

- _____ behavior

---

_____

_____

_____

_____

_____

_____

_____

_____

_____

_____

_____

_____

_____

_____

**6 minutes**     ## Video Segment 2: "Set Up a Detention Hall"

> Remind the participants that key points from the video segment can be found on pages 117–18 of the Participant's Guide if they would like to review them at a later time.

> View Video Segment 2: "Set Up a Detention Hall."

Now let's see how boundaries are protected and enforced by logical consequences that we establish. Please turn to page 119.

**5 minutes**     ## A Few More Thoughts on . . . Setting Appropriate Consequences

> Participant's Guide page 119.

Stating your boundary is not enough—you also have to lay down a consequence and stick to it. Consequences are God's school of discipline (Hebrews 12:11); they are the realities you set up for when a boundary is crossed again. You will need to determine appropriate consequences for infractions that keep occurring. The punishment needs to fit the crime.

➡ Here are four guidelines for setting appropriate consequences:

1.  Be motivated by LOVE and truth, not REVENGE. Think of consequences as protecting you and giving her a chance to change.
2.  AVOID the ultimate consequence: breaking off the relationship prematurely. Breaking up is not truly a consequence because it ends rather than cures a relationship.
3.  Think EMPATHICALLY. Put yourself in your date's shoes. How would you feel with various consequences?
4.  Use REALITY as your guide. Make the consequences fit, as much as possible, with natural consequences. Get yourself out of the way as much as possible so your date doesn't see you as the problem, but sees his relationship with reality as the problem.

Please turn to page 120.

# PLANNING NOTES

_____

_____

_____

_____

_____

_____

_____

_____

_____

_____

_____

_____

---

## VIDEO SEGMENT
### *Set Up a Detention Hall*

- Though no one has the power to fix anyone else, you do have the power to respond in healthy ways to your date when problems arise.

- Some conflict is normal. Problems, including boundary conflicts, are a normal part of relationships.

- Don't wait to set a limit until there is a huge problem or crisis in your love life. Boundaries should be woven into the fabric of your daily life and relationships.

- See boundaries as tools for diagnosing the character of your date and of the relationship. Basically, think about boundaries as preserving the relationship, not ending it.

- Approach your date from a stance of love, respect, and mutuality. Be very specific with your date about the boundary problem.

- Have these seven things in place as you go through the boundary-setting process.

  1. *Stay connected* to good people who will stand by you when conflicts arise.
  2. *Avoid reactive friends* who idealize you as an innocent victim or who are critical and judgmental of you. Find mature people who are "for" both of you and can see both sides of the issue.
  3. *Expect negative reactions.* Don't be surprised by anger or defensiveness, but demand respect.
  4. *Empathize with the struggle*, acknowledging that what you are requiring is difficult.
  5. *Be patient* and allow time for God's process to take hold. But recognize also that patience has an end; it does not wait forever without a good reason.
  6. *Question his motives.* It is important that your date be changing because of his relationship with God, because it

---

    is the right thing to do, and because he doesn't want to hurt you—and not changing simply because he wants you back.

7. *Provide a way back to normal relationships* by letting your date know that the consequences are not necessarily permanent. But stay out of the parental role—be his equal!

- If you have boundary struggles with someone you are involved with, it makes sense to set up consequences aimed at dealing with the problem.

- Everyone needs to be involved in the process of spiritual growth. This means being in a process in which the person brings his struggles, weaknesses, and vulnerabilities to God and some safe people on an ongoing basis.

---

## A FEW MORE THOUGHTS ON . . .
## SETTING APPROPRIATE CONSEQUENCES

    Here are four guidelines for setting appropriate consequences:

1. Be motivated by _____ and truth, not _____.
   Think of consequences as protecting you and giving your date a chance to change.

2. _____ the ultimate consequence: breaking off the relationship prematurely. Breaking up is not truly a consequence because it ends rather than cures a relationship.

3. Think _____. Put yourself in your date's shoes. How would you feel with various consequences?

4. Use _____ as your guide. Make the consequences fit, as much as possible, with natural consequences. Get yourself out of the way as much as possible so your date doesn't see you as the problem, but sees his relationship with reality as the problem.

## 10 minutes   *Let's Talk: Boundaries Are Not Consequences*

> Participant's Guide page 120.

### Directions

1. I will divide you into four groups and assign each group a scenario from page 120.
2. Considering the scenario to which you've been assigned, answer the two questions at the bottom of the page.
3. You will have 5 minutes to complete this exercise.

> Divide the class into four groups and assign each a scenario from page 120 in the Participant's Guide. Let the participants know when there is 1 minute remaining. Call the group back together after 5 minutes.

## 2 MINUTES   SUMMARY

We've looked at three ways you can solve dating problems when your date is the problem. First, you can say no to disrespect. Second, you can nip in the bud inappropriate behavior. And, third, you can use natural consequences to maintain healthy and effective boundaries. This week's "Boundary Building," found on page 121, will help you take these steps.

## 1 minute   *Closing Prayer*

Loving and wise God, we are so glad you love us and care about our dating relationships! Help us to live by your Golden Rule, by your command to treat others the way we want to be treated. Please forgive us when we are disrespectful—and please help us be wise and bold when we are treated disrespectfully.

We also ask, Lord, that you would make us people who can hear truth and act on it, turning to you for growth and change. Give us courage and wisdom to confront things that are important and the grace to forgive and tolerate when that is appropriate. May we live out our dating relationships in the light of truth.

Finally, Lord God, we ask you to grant us wisdom and guidance first to choose dates and later as we deal with the inevitable conflicts. We need your compassion and strength as we establish consequences to support our boundaries. We need your people to support us in the good and the bad of dating. And we need your transforming power in our own journey of spiritual growth. We need you to be part of our dating life—and we thank you in advance for your faithfulness, your goodness, and your presence with us always. In Jesus' name. Amen.

# PLANNING NOTES

_____

_____

_____

_____

_____

_____

_____

_____

_____

_____

_____

_____

_____

_____

_____

_____

_____

_____

_____

_____

_____

_____

_____

_____

---

120      *Boundaries in Dating Paticipant's Guide*

### LET'S TALK
#### *Boundaries Are Not Consequences*

**DIRECTIONS**

1. The leader will divide you into four groups and assign each group a scenario from below.
2. Considering the scenario to which you've been assigned, answer the two questions at the bottom of the page.
3. You will have 5 minutes to complete this exercise.

**DATING SCENARIOS**

1. Your date is always late.
2. Your date wants to stay in touch with former boyfriends/ girlfriends.
3. Your boyfriend/girlfriend wants to borrow money from you.
4. Your boyfriend/girlfriend has a secret drug or alcohol problem.

   What might be some appropriate consequences that would improve this situation? List two or three.

Review the four guidelines for setting appropriate consequences. How did the consequences you just established for your hypothetical situation measure up? What tweaking is needed to make those consequences more appropriate?

---

Session Nine: *Solving Dating Problems When Your Date is the Problem*   121

## Boundary Building

Look again at the list on page 116 of some things in a relationship that should not be tolerated for very long.

1. When have you been guilty of these behaviors, if any? What does that fact reveal about the growing up you need to do—and what steps will you take toward a more godly and mature character?
2. When, in the past, have you tolerated any of these behaviors? What would you now do differently in that situation?
3. What appropriate and effective consequences might you establish in each situation you just referred to?

Also, take time to answer the "For personal reflection" question in the "What Cures Disrespect" exercise.

## Suggested Reading

For more thoughts on this session's topics, read chapters 15, 16, and 18 in *Boundaries in Dating:* "Say No to Disrespect," "Nip It in the Bud," and "Set Up a Detention Hall." For a more thorough self-evaluation, look at chapters 15, 16, and 18 in the *Boundaries in Dating Workbook*.

# Session Ten

# Appropriate Physical Limits— and a Few Closing Words

## BEFORE YOU LEAD

### Key Points

- God wants people to reserve sex for marriage (1 Thessalonians 4:3–8).
- First Thessalonians 4:3–8 contains five reasons why God calls for sexual abstinence outside marriage: (1) we are to live holy and honorable lives, (2) we are to live with self-control, (3) we are not to give in to passionate lust, (4) we are to avoid wronging someone, and (5) we are to accept God and his rules as we live in submission to him.
- Sexuality is a part of God's good creation. But as you embrace your sexuality, do so with self-control, sanctity, high esteem, lovingly and not lustfully, sacrificially and not "wronging" someone, and in submission to God.
- If you have already said yes instead of no to sex outside of marriage, God has gracious words of love and forgiveness for you.
- Boundaries in dating is about becoming a truthful, caring, responsible, and free person who encourages growth in those with whom you are in contact. It is about how to better conduct your dating life to develop love, freedom, and responsibility in both you and whomever you are dating.
- Six critical measures of a good dating relationship will help you make sure that the good things God has designed in dating are actually occurring: (1) Is dating growing you up? (2) Is dating bringing you closer to God? (3) Are you more able to have good relationships? (4) Are you picking better dates over time? (5) Are you a better potential mate? and (6) Are you enjoying the ride?

## *Synopsis*

God wants people to reserve sex for marriage. While for many people, both inside and outside of the church, this does not make sense, those who have reaped the consequences of the pain that sex outside of marriage can bring know there are good reasons to wait.

Dr. Cloud and Dr. Townsend begin by looking at 1 Thessalonians 4:3–8. Here God gives five reasons for sexual abstinence outside marriage. First, Paul calls God's people to "control [their] body in a way that is holy and honorable" (v. 4). *Holiness* means "purity" and "being set aside for a high purpose," and *honor* means things like "dignity, precious, of high price or value, or high esteem." So, first, God is saying that sex is not a casual thing. Like other things of high value, to spend sex casually or unwisely is foolish, and you will be cheated in the end.

Paul also says, "Each of you should learn to control his own body" (v. 4). Control of one's own body is a sign that a person is capable of delay of gratification and self-control, which are prerequisites of the ability to love. That's the second reason God reserves sex for marriage.

The third reason is related. Paul teaches against passionate lust (v. 5), a lust for that which is forbidden outside of marriage. A healthy person is someone who is integrated; whose body, soul, and mind are all working together. If someone has not married you, then they have given less than 100 percent of themselves and should get less than 100 percent of your body. Also, passionate lust splits you from your real heart, your mind, your values, and the life you truly desire. Lust gets momentary fulfillment at the expense of lasting gain.

Fourth, Paul also teaches that when sex occurs outside of marriage, someone is always wronged (v. 6). When someone sleeps with a person to whom he or she is not married, he or she is hurting that person. If you say you are a person of love, then you won't wrong someone you love. You will wait. And vice versa, do not allow anyone else to wrong you. Love waits to give, but lust can't wait to get.

And, fifth, Paul teaches us that the authority for sexuality belongs not to us, but to God. There are few better tests for whether or not someone lives a life in submission to God than what he or she does with their sexuality. God wants to be accepted as he really is, rules and all. When someone rewrites God's values, they are not accepting who he really is. So be sure you're trusting a person who truly trusts God. If he or she is, that person will uphold God's value of sex within marriage.

One more point. It is difficult to keep someone out of your heart who has invaded your body. That in itself is another reason to say no to sex outside of marriage.

You may agree wholeheartedly with what the Lord calls you to do and with what Dr. Cloud and Dr. Townsend teach—but you may have already said yes instead of no to sex outside of marriage. God has gracious words of love and forgiveness for you. If you ask God to forgive you through Jesus, he sees you as a completely new person. You are clean, washed with pure water. Whatever you might have done is forgotten and put away as the east is from the west. As Paul says, "there is no . . . condemnation" for those who have asked for the forgiveness that Jesus gives (Romans 8:1). If you know you are forgiven, that clean slate is a powerful boundary as you walk in the state of being guilt-free.

In closing, here are six critical measures of a good relationship to help you make sure that the good things God has designed in dating are actually occurring:

1. Is dating growing you up?
2. Is dating bringing you closer to God?
3. Are you more able to have good relationships?
4. Are you picking better dates over time?
5. Are you a better potential mate?
6. Are you enjoying the ride?

## Recommended Reading

"Set Appropriate Physical Limits" (chapter 17) and the conclusion of *Boundaries in Dating*

# *Session Ten*

# Appropriate Physical Limits— and a Few Closing Words

## 4 MINUTES   INTRODUCTION

### 1 minute   *Welcome*

> Call the group together and welcome the participants to Session 10, "Appropriate Physical Limits — and a Few Closing Words."

### 1 minute   *Opening Prayer*

Lord God, as we've met together, we've learned much about your plan for our lives, specifically for our dating lives. Now, as we begin our last session, we ask—as we have all along—that you would bless us with hearts that hear your Word, that understand its call on our lives, and that are soft beneath your transforming touch. We pray that we would receive your truth and let it change us and free us to be the people you want us to be. We pray in Jesus' name. Amen.

### 2 minutes   *Review and Overview*

> Participant's Guide page 123.

We've covered a lot of ground in this series. We started by defining healthy boundaries and spent some time focusing on the essential boundary of truth. We considered how to take God on a date and how to establish boundaries around our wish for a relationship and around our past. Next we looked at what traits we can and can't live with in a

160

# PLANNING NOTES

---

*Session Ten*

## Appropriate Physical Limits— and a Few Closing Words

### OVERVIEW

In this session you will

- Look closely at 1 Thessalonians 4:3–8, God's "big rule" of reserving sex for marriage.
- Consider five reasons why God calls for sexual abstinence outside of marriage.
- Hear gracious words about the forgiveness available to you if you have already said yes to sex outside of marriage.
- Evaluate six critical measures of a good dating relationship to help you make sure that the good things God has designed for life are actually occurring in dating.

123

date, at the dynamics of a relationship between opposites, and at the differences between friendships and dating relationships. And we just finished three sessions in which we talked about how to solve dating problems, whether we are the problem or our date is.

Let's turn to page 123.

→ Today, before we wrap up the series, we're going to talk about why and how to establish appropriate physical limits in your dating relationships. We will look closely at 1 Thessalonians 4:3–8, God's "big rule" of reserving sex for marriage. We'll consider five reasons why God calls for sexual abstinence outside of marriage. We'll hear gracious words about the forgiveness available to you if you have already said yes to sex outside of marriage. And we'll evaluate six critical measures of a good dating relationship to help you make sure that the good things God has designed for life are actually occurring in dating.

Dr. Cloud and Dr. Townsend will get us started.

# 45 MINUTES DISCOVERY

## *9 minutes*           *Video Segment 1: "The Big Rule—and Why"*

> Remind the participants that key points from the video segment can be found on pages 124–25 in their Participant's Guide if they would like to review them at a later time.

> View Video Segment 1: "The Big Rule—and Why."

In the 1 Thessalonians passage discussed in the video, Paul gives five reasons for sexual abstinence outside of marriage—we are to live holy and honorable lives; we are to live with self-control; we are not to give in to passionate lust; we are to avoid wronging someone; and we are to accept God and his rules as we live in submission to him.

As you embrace your sexuality, do so with self-control, sanctity, high esteem, lovingly and not lustfully, sacrificially and not "wronging" someone, and in submission to God. Then, when you are dating, you will have built in some very good limits and expression of your sexual person. You will know, for example, how far is too far. You cannot act out inappropriately with these guidelines in place. They are appropriately confining.

# PLANNING NOTES

_____

_____

_____

_____

_____

_____

_____

_____

_____

_____

_____

*Session Ten*

## Appropriate Physical Limits— and a Few Closing Words

### OVERVIEW

In this session you will

- Look closely at 1 Thessalonians 4:3–8, God's "big rule" of reserving sex for marriage.
- Consider five reasons why God calls for sexual abstinence outside of marriage.
- Hear gracious words about the forgiveness available to you if you have already said yes to sex outside of marriage.
- Evaluate six critical measures of a good dating relationship to help you make sure that the good things God has designed for life are actually occurring in dating.

123

---

### VIDEO SEGMENT
#### *The Big Rule—and Why*

- God wants people to reserve sex for marriage. This rule is found, among other places, in 1 Thessalonians 4:3–8:

    It is God's will that you should be sanctified: that you should avoid sexual immorality; that each of you should learn to control his own body in a way that is holy and honorable, not in passionate lust like the heathen, who do not know God; and that in this matter no one should wrong his brother or take advantage of him. The Lord will punish men for all such sins, as we have already told you and warned you. For God did not call us to be impure, but to live a holy life. Therefore he who rejects this instruction does not reject man but God, who gives you his Holy Spirit.

- This statement of God's rule contains five reasons why he calls for sexual abstinence outside marriage. First, Paul calls God's people to "control [their] body in a way that is holy and honorable" (1 Thessalonians 4:4). *Holiness* means "purity" and "being set aside for a high purpose," and *honor* means things like "dignity, precious, of high price or value, or high esteem." God is saying that sex is not a casual thing. To spend sex casually or unwisely is foolish, and you will be cheated in the end.

- Paul also says, "Each of you should learn to control his own body" (1 Thessalonians 4:4). Control of one's own body is a sign that a person is capable of delay of gratification and self-control, which are prerequisites of the ability to love.

- Paul teaches against passionate lust (1 Thessalonians 4:5), a lust for that which is forbidden outside of marriage. Passionate lust splits you from your real heart, your mind, your values, and the life you truly desire. Lust gets momentary fulfillment at the expense of lasting gain.

---

- Paul also teaches that when sex occurs outside of marriage, someone is always wronged (1 Thessalonians 4:6). When someone sleeps with a person to whom he or she is not married, he or she is hurting that person. If you say you are a person of love, then you won't wrong someone you love. You will wait. And vice versa, do not allow anyone else to wrong you. Love waits to give, but lust can't wait to get.

- Paul teaches us that the authority for sexuality belongs not to us, but to God. God wants to be accepted as he really is, rules and all. When someone rewrites God's values, they are not accepting who he really is.

- It is difficult to keep someone out of your heart who has invaded your body. That in itself is another reason to say no to sex outside of marriage.

- Sexuality is a part of God's good creation. But as you embrace your sexuality, do so with self-control, sanctity, high esteem, lovingly and not lustfully, sacrificially and not "wronging" someone, and in submission to God.

In order to make these rules more a part of your thinking, let's take some time to work through the following exercise. Please turn to page 126.

**15 minutes**

## On Your Own: Five Reasons for the Big Rule

> Participant's Guide page 126.

### Directions

On your own, work through the questions listed on page 126–29. What you don't get to will be your "Boundary Building" exercise this week. You will have 15 minutes to complete this exercise. Any questions?

**8 minutes**

## A Few More Thoughts on . . . the Boundary of Forgiveness

> Participant's Guide page 130.

You may agree wholeheartedly with what the Lord calls you to do and with what Dr. Cloud and Dr. Townsend have taught—but you may have already said yes instead of no to sex outside of marriage. If so, God has gracious words of love and forgiveness for you. Please turn to page 130 and follow along.

➜ If you ask God to FORGIVE you through Jesus, he sees you as a completely new person. You are clean, washed with pure water. Whatever you might have done is forgotten and put away as the east is from the west. As Paul says, "there is no. . .CONDEMNATION" for those who have asked for the forgiveness that Jesus gives (Romans 8:1).

Your past failure does not have to doom you to further sexual brokenness. Just because you have fallen in the past does not mean that you have ruined yourself and cannot START OVER. You can become clean again. And as you do, you can COMMIT to remaining pure and enjoying all the benefits of that state:

- You can develop the INNER life and your ability to LOVE.
- You can know if someone really loves you.
- You can learn how to DELAY gratification and GIVE to others.
- You can have your underlying splits, needs, and hurts HEALED and fulfilled so that you will not have unsatisfying relationships.

## ON YOUR OWN
### *Five Reasons for the Big Rule*

**DIRECTIONS**

On your own, work through the questions below. What you don't get to will be your "Boundary Building" exercise this week. You will have 15 minutes to complete this exercise.

**Holy and honorable.** Sex is set apart for a purpose and has great value. It is for a lifelong commitment and needs to be esteemed. In a physical and spiritual sense, it is all you can give someone. Therefore, it should not be given away lightly.

1. What differences exist between a break up when the couple was sleeping together and a break up when the couple wasn't? Answer this question based on either what you've seen or what you've experienced.

2. Because sex and the heart are connected, people often feel as if they lose a part of themselves when a lover ends a relationship. Why do so many of us learn that the hard way—from our own experience rather than from people who have gone before us?

**Self-control.** Choose someone who can delay gratification for the sake of you and the relationship. Boundaries with sex are a surefire test to know if someone loves you for you.

3. A committed relationship calls for sacrifice. In friendships as well as dating relationships, what kinds of sacrifices have you seen made—or perhaps made yourself—in any of the following areas?

Time

Money

Getting one's own way

Working out conflict

4. What kind of sacrifices are involved in respecting boundaries about sex?

5. What is a good response to "If you love me, you will [have sex]"?

**Passionate lust.** Instead of expressing love through sex, the luster replaces love with sex. Lust gets momentary fulfillment at the expense of lasting gain. Furthermore—as countless married people have found out—the person they married who could not wait was incapable of real relationship.

6. Lusters have divided souls and do not develop deeper aspects of themselves which are necessary for a lasting relationship. What undeveloped skills can sex outside of marriage keep a person from dealing with? What activities can sex replace?

7. Your sexual abstinence is a great way to find out how fulfilled you are as a person. When, if ever, have you used sex to replace relationship? What does that action tell you about your deep longings and unhealed hurts?

**Wronging someone.** If you say you are a person of love, then you won't wrong someone you love. You will wait. And vice versa, do not allow anyone else to wrong you. Love waits to give.

8. If you have slept with someone outside of marriage, which of the following hurts have you experienced as a result?

- Your soul and body split: your body gave 100 percent, and your soul was connected to some lesser degree.
- You cheapened a very precious part of yourself and someone else.
- You caused a person to not develop deeper aspects of relatedness and spirituality.
- You came between a person and God.
- You helped a person deny hurt and pain.
- You used someone for your own pleasure and lust, and that is a long way from love.
- While you used them, you kept them from finding someone who will truly value them.
- You set them up for heartbreak and devastation if you break up and take with you something so precious.

9. If you have pressured someone to sleep with you outside of marriage, what hurts listed in question 8 might you have inflicted? What, if anything, have you done to seek forgiveness—God's as well as that person's?

**Accepting God.** God wants to be accepted as he really is, rules and all. When someone rewrites his values, they are not accepting who he really is. So be sure you're trusting a person who truly trusts God. If he or she is, that person will uphold God's value of sex within marriage.

10. Why is it important—for a dating relationship now and for a possible marriage in the future—to see whether a person submits to the Lord? Put differently, what kinds of problems will arise if your date submits only when God's way doesn't interfere with his or her desires?

11. What does the litmus test of your sexuality tell you about yourself, your spirituality, and your submission to the God of the Bible rather than to a God you're re-creating to fit your needs and desires? Are you walking humbly with your God (Micah 6:8)? What repentance is in order?

- You can finally give up being God and allow him to be GOD for you.

If you know you are forgiven, that clean slate is a powerful BOUNDARY. Dating can now be about building deeper things than a one-night experience. It can be a place of GROWTH instead of brokenness.

So ask God for his forgiveness now. If you do not know Jesus, ask him to be your Lord. Turn to him in faith and he will cleanse you. And then walk in that state of being guilt-free. It is a place of strength, and you will find yourself able to wait on the real thing.

## *3 minutes*     *Video Segment 2: "Critical Measures of a Good Dating Relationship"*

We have a few more minutes together, and I want to use that time to hear some closing thoughts from Dr. Cloud and Dr. Townsend.

> Remind the participants that key points from the video segment can be found on page 131 of their Participants' Guide if they would like to review them at a later time.

> View Video Segment 2: "Critical Measures of a Good Dating Relationship."

## *10 minutes*     *Let's Talk: How Are You Doing?*

> Participant's Guide page 132.

Boundaries in dating is about becoming a truthful, caring, responsible and free person who encourages growth in those with whom you are in contact. It is about how to better conduct your dating life to develop love, freedom, and responsibility in both you and whomever you are dating. So let's talk for a few minutes about how we're doing. Please turn to page 132.

### Directions

Pair up with someone sitting near you and discuss the questions found on page 132. You will have 10 minutes to complete this exercise. Any questions?

> Let the participants know when there is 1 minute remaining. Call the group back together after 10 minutes.

# PLANNING NOTES

_____

_____

_____

_____

_____

_____

_____

_____

_____

_____

_____

## A FEW MORE THOUGHTS ON . . . THE BOUNDARY OF FORGIVENESS

If you ask God to _____ you through Jesus, he sees you as a completely new person. You are clean, washed with pure water. Whatever you might have done is forgotten and put away as the east is from the west. As Paul says, "there is...no _____" for those who have asked for the forgiveness that Jesus gives (Romans 8:1).

Your past failure does not have to doom you to further sexual brokenness. Just because you have fallen in the past does not mean that you have ruined yourself and cannot _____ _____. You can become clean again. And as you do, you can _____ to remaining pure and enjoying all the benefits of that state:

- You can develop the _____ life and your ability to _____.
- You can know if someone really loves you.
- You can learn how to _____ gratification and _____ to others.
- You can have your underlying splits, needs, and hurts _____ and fulfilled so that you will not have unsatisfying relationships.
- You can finally give up being God and allow him to be _____ for you.

If you know you are forgiven, that clean slate is a powerful _____. Dating can now be about building deeper things than a one-night experience. It can be a place of _____ instead of brokenness.

## VIDEO SEGMENT
### Critical Measures of a Good Dating Relationship

- Learning to have good boundaries in dating is work and takes some time, but it pays off as you understand how to better conduct your dating life to develop love, freedom, and responsibility in both you and whomever you are dating.
- Boundaries in dating is about becoming a truthful, caring, responsible, and free person who encourages growth in those with whom you are in contact. The following six critical measures are meant to make sure that the good things God has designed in dating are actually occurring:
  1. Is dating growing me up?
  2. Is dating bringing me closer to God?
  3. Am I more able to have good relationships?
  4. Am I picking better dates over time?
  5. Am I a better potential mate?
  6. Am I enjoying the ride?

## LET'S TALK
### How Are You Doing?

**DIRECTIONS**

Pair up with someone sitting near you and discuss the six questions found on page 131 and the questions below. You will have 10 minutes to complete this exercise.

1. If you've been dating, what aspects of your dating are you pleased with? What points do you want to work on?

2. Whether you have an active dating life or are about to start dating or start dating again, what specific goals do you have for your dating life?

3. Whatever your situation, what about this book's perspective on dating has convicted you? Challenged you? Encouraged you?

## 2 MINUTES     SUMMARY

I trust that you've found this *Boundaries in Dating* series worthwhile. And I want to remind you that the truths we've been discussing, the insights we've been sharing, and the skills we've been sharpening are important for life. I encourage you to find some safe friends, perhaps from this group, to keep you growing and accountable to the things you've been learning and practicing. I also invite you to continue the boundary-building work you've begun. Specifically, this week's "Boundary Building" exercise asks you to finish working on the "On Your Own: Five Reasons for the Big Rule" questions as well as on the "Let's Talk: How Are You Doing?" questions we just touched on. Again, assignments like these are actually projects for life, pointing us toward health and growth and living the way God has designed us to live. Let's close our time together by asking his blessing.

## 1 minute     *Closing Prayer*

Almighty and Creator God, after this session, we're understanding better than ever how your lordship is key to our sexuality. Forgive us for our pride that has caused us to doubt and even refuse to submit to your guidelines for our sexuality. And forgive us for any sexual brokenness we've chosen or caused. Help us to receive your forgiveness and to submit to your will for us in this—and every other—area of our life. And please help us to look to you for strength as we walk the path of purity you call us to. We ask for sensitivity to your loving hand of wisdom, guidance, and protection on all our dating relationships and activities. In Jesus' name. Amen.

# PLANNING NOTES

## Boundary Building

Continue the boundary building work you've begun by completing the "On Your Own: Five Reasons for the Big Rule" questions. Remember that assignments like these are actually projects for life, pointing you to health and growth and living the way God has designed you to live.

## Suggested Reading

For more thoughts on this session's topics, read "Set Appropriate Physical Limits" (chapter 17) and the conclusion of *Boundaries in Dating*. For a more thorough self-evaluation, look at chapter 17 and the conclusion in the *Boundaries in Dating Workbook*.

# *Appendix* — Script

## SESSION 1

## Video Segment 1: "Dating: People Problems and Potential Benefits"

*Person 1:* My friends leave me all kinds of messages. "Are you still alive?" "Have you dropped off the planet?" I mean, I can't help spending all my time with him. My real friends would understand.

*Person 2:* Whenever she's around, I have to have her closer. And holding her in my arms—it's the best feeling ever! I know I'm in love.

*Person 3:* We were so much alike, we could finish each other's sentences! We liked to go to the same restaurants; we liked to do the same things. But he just won't commit! I don't get it.

*Person 4:* My hair was everywhere. I had no makeup on. I couldn't answer the door. I couldn't let him see me like that. He would never ask me out again.

*Person 5:* On the first date, I knew she was the one! I didn't want her dating anyone else—and I certainly wasn't interested in anyone else, even though I hardly knew her.

*Person 6:* I hate being alone. The couples all around me—they look so happy. Why isn't God letting me find someone to date?

*HC:* Do you see yourself in any of these people? If so, you've bumped up against some common problems in dating. These problems can be discouraging to that point that some people stop dating all together. Well, I'm Dr. Henry Cloud, and I believe in dating. I don't think you need to kiss dating good-bye at all.

*JT:* I'm Dr. John Townsend, and I agree. Oh, dating has its problems. We can be kidnapped or distracted from important life tasks. We can lose who we are. We can miss out on the good things that come with being single.

*HC:* These are problems, but these problems point not to a problem with dating, but to a problem with people. Human problems are matters of the heart, the soul, one's orientation towards God, and a whole host of other maturity issues. Spiritual growth is the cure for such immaturity. That's why learning how to love, following God, being honest and responsible, treating others as you would want to be treated, developing self-control, and building a fulfilling life will ensure better dating.

*JT:* In this series, we'll address each of the problems we have just reviewed by looking at the lack of appropriate structure within, among other things, a person's character, their support system, their values, and their relationship with God. In other words, a lack of boundaries. As we talk in greater detail about dating problems like these seven, we'll also show the boundaries that will cure them. God gives us principles to guide us in life. Because we can trust in his ways, we're free to grow and develop a life as we mature. We don't have to avoid life (and that includes dating), and we don't have to avoid maturity.

*HC:* In fact, we go beyond thinking that dating is something to be avoided. We see several benefits in dating. Dating gives people the opportunity to learn about themselves and others and relationships in a safe context. It also provides a context to work through issues in your life. And thirdly, dating helps build relationship skills. It can also help heal and repair things that hurt your soul. Dating is relational and it has value because of that reason in and of itself. It also lets someone learn what he or she likes in the opposite sex before getting too serious. Dating can give you a context to learn sexual self-control and other kinds of really important delays of gratification.

*JT:* Dating can be a great time of life, but it must be balanced with God's boundaries of what's good. When dating's done well, it can lead to great fruits in the life of the teen and the adult single. If you take this series seriously, seek God as deeply as you know how, and you establish a healthy community of friends to support you in the process. If you keep God's boundaries for living a fulfilled but holy life, then dating can be a great thing.

## *Video Segment 2: "Freedom, Responsibility, and Boundaries"*

*Julie:* So Heather, how are things going with Todd?

*Heather:* The same as the last time you asked! He's the greatest! I mean, he's loving, responsible, and fun! We have such a good time when we're together. I could marry him in a heartbeat!

*Julie:* So what's the problem?

*Heather:* It's just that when I start talking about getting serious, he changes the subject.

*Julie:* Yikes. That one.

*Heather:* Yeah.

*Julie:* So what can you do to get him. . .moving forward?

*Heather: (frustrated, hurt, discouraged)* I don't know. What can I do. . .hold him at gunpoint until he commits?

*JT:* Heather has made Todd a high emotional priority in her life. And it's no wonder that she's frustrated. You see, she and Todd are clearly on different tracks. She's hurt because her love feels unrequited; she's discouraged because she's invested a lot of her heart, her time, and her energy in that relationship. You see, Heather has given up activities that she enjoyed and relationships that she valued. She tried to become the kind of person she thought Todd would be attracted to. And now it looks like this investment is going nowhere.

*HC:* You know, many of the struggles people experience in dating—struggles like Heather's experiencing—are caused by some problem in the areas of freedom or responsibility. Now, by freedom, we mean your ability to make choices based on your values, rather than choosing out of fear or guilt. Free people make commitments because they feel like it's the right thing to do, and they're wholehearted about it.

By responsibility, we mean your ability to do the tasks in keeping the relationship healthy and loving, as well as being able to say no to things you shouldn't be responsible for. You see, responsible people shoulder their part of the dating relationship, but they don't tolerate harmful or inappropriate behavior.

*JT:* We believe that healthy boundaries are the key to preserving freedom, responsibility, and ultimately love in your dating life. Establishing and keeping good limits can do a great deal to not only cure a bad relationship, but make a good one even better.

*Question from audience:* Yeah, what do you mean when you use the word *boundaries?*

*JT:* Good question, and it's a question that we need to answer before we start, because how we approach that word will have a direct effect on problems that arise from freedom and responsibility in dating.

*HC:* Simply put, a boundary's a property line. Just as a physical fence marks out where your yard ends and your neighbor's begins, a personal boundary distinguishes what is your emotional or personal property and what belongs to someone else. When another person tries to control you, or tries to get too close to you, or asks you to do something that you don't think is right, your boundary's been crossed.

*JT:* Boundaries serve two important functions. First, they *define* us. They show us what we are and what we're not; and what we agree with and what we disagree with; what we love and what we hate. God has many clear boundaries. He loves the world; he loves cheerful givers. He hates haughty eyes and a lying tongue. As people made in his image, we also are to be honest and truthful about what we are and about what we are not.

*HC:* The second function of boundaries is that they *protect* us. Boundaries keep good things in and bad things out. When we don't have clear limits, we can expose ourselves to unhealthy or destructive influences and people. And boundaries protect us by letting others know what you will and what you won't tolerate.

*JT:* Boundaries are basically a fence protecting your property. Now in dating, what's your property is your soul. Boundaries surround the life that God's given you to maintain and mature, so that you can become the person he created you to be. You and only you are responsible for what's inside your boundaries—things like your love, and your emotions, and your values, and your behaviors. Your own inability to have control over these parts of yourself is the real problem. But boundaries are the key to keeping your soul safe, and protected, and growing. Remember, you're not being mean when you say no. Instead, you may be saving yourself or even the relationship from injury.

# SESSION 2

## *Video Segment 1: "Standing on Quicksand"*

*Woman telling her story:* You know, I never thought I could feel greater pain than I did when Tom first told me about his affair. I was devastated to learn that I'd been sharing my husband with another woman—and he'd been sharing himself with someone else. I couldn't believe it. But there I was, living this surreal nightmare. The pain, the rage...It was awful...Then, just when I was allowing God to deal with the pain, even healing to the point where I wanted to reconcile with Tom, the roof caved in again, and things got even worse. Right when he told me that he'd been with her more often than he had told me at first. It wasn't just two trade shows in the fall. There were lunchtime encounters and after-hours late nights through December. It was as though the affair was happening all over again—but worse. This time there was lying on top of lying and deception. It was more than I could take. I felt like I was standing on quicksand. And I just couldn't live in the same house with that man. So we're separated again, and I realized and I learned that where there is deception, there is no relationship. He lied so much I just didn't know who he was anymore.

*HC:* "Where there is deception, there is no relationship." She learned this important lesson the hard way. Honesty is the bedrock of dating and marriage.

*JT:* I've seen relationships undermined by deception in many areas—finances, work performance, substance abuse, and many other topics. The lying and deception are destructive whatever the topic. The real problem is that when you're with someone who is deceptive, you never know what reality is. You're not standing on firm ground, and the ground can shift at any moment. As one woman said, "Deception makes you question everything."

*HC:* There are many different ways to deceive someone in the world of dating. Let's look at six of the more common ones. First, there's deception about your relationship. For example, Karen liked Matt a lot, but he was getting more serious than she was in his feelings for her. But Karen knew this and ignored her discomfort, and she continued to go out with Matt as he fell more and more in love with her. When Karen eventually broke off the relationship, Matt was devastated. Disillusioned, he didn't date again for a long, long time.

It's one thing to have loved and lost, but it's is another thing to have loved and been lied to. So don't lead someone on. Matt would've been a lot better off if he had been hurt earlier. Karen deceived him about the nature of the relationship itself.

*JT:* Second, there's deception about being friends. Sometimes people are deceptive about their true intentions while they're acting like a friend. Now, certainly you don't have to put all of your cards on the table very early when you have a crush on a person. But being sneaky and being cautious are two very different things. Don't act like a friend if you're not. And only you know for sure.

*HC:* Third, there's deception about other people. Sometimes people deceive each other about the nature of other people in their lives. They may act like this other person is "just a friend," when there is more of a history, or maybe even more in the present, than is being said.

*JT:* Next, remember that you will have a good relationship to the degree that you're able to be clear and honest about everything. If you like a certain kind of music, or church, or activity, say so. Now that doesn't mean you can't die to your own wishes to please someone else. But don't be afraid to be yourself. Don't be deceptive about who you are. Instead, be honest, have some differences, and enjoy the trip.

*HC:* Fifth, some people tell lies not about feelings, relationships, or personal preferences, but about reality itself. Be careful and watch out for factual lies—like lies about finances, or substance abuse, maybe the person's whereabouts, or maybe seeing them with someone else, their past, or the nature of their achievements. Lying about reality places your relationship on a really shaky foundation.

*JT:* Finally, there's deception about hurt and conflict. If there's a problem in some way a date has treated you, or some hurt you've suffered, you must be honest. Being honest resolves the hurt or the conflict. And when you're honest, you will see by how the other person responds whether a long-term, satisfactory relationship is even possible. People who can handle confrontation and feedback are the very ones who can make relationships work. Honesty over hurt and conflict creates intimacy, and it also divides people into the wise and the foolish. But being honest is totally up to you.

## Video Segment 2: *"Honesty: The Best Boundary of All"*

*HC:* Where there is deception, there is no relationship. So why do people lie? Well, some people lie out of shame or guilt, or fear of conflict or loss of love, and other kinds of fears when it would be a lot easier to tell the truth. And they want to be honest, but for one reason or another they can't quite pull it off. They fear the other person's anger or maybe even a loss of love.

*JT:* In the second category of liars are those people who lie as a way of operating and deceive others for their own selfish ends. There is no fear or defensiveness involved. It's just plain old lying for self-interest.

*HC:* You'll have to ask yourself if you want to take the risk and if you want to do the work with that first type of liar. But the second kind of liar is a definite no-go. Tell him or her good-bye and save yourself a lot of heartache.

*JT:* Bottom line: We think you should spend your time and your heart on honest people. And that's because we believe that truthfulness is the basis for almost everything. You should have an absolute zero-tolerance policy when it comes to deception. Lying should have no place in your life. Listen to King David's tough stance on lying: "No one who practices deceit will dwell in my house; no one who speaks falsely will stand in my presence" (Ps. 101:7).

*HC:* David was clear, straightforward, strict—and, we think, right on. Don't tolerate lying, period. Now that doesn't mean if you're lied to once in a relationship that the whole relationship has to be over—especially if the person wasn't being totally clear and direct about certain preferences or desires. And probably every human being is growing in the ability to be direct and completely vulnerable with things like feelings and deeper parts of the heart. But don't tolerate deception or lying when it happens. Make a rule: "I have to be with someone who is honest with me about what they're thinking or feeling."

*JT:* But if you are two-timed, lied to about facts, with a substance abuser in denial, or otherwise deceived, we more than caution you about going forward. In many instances, lying like this is indicative of a serious character problem, and this problem doesn't change without major hurt for many people along the way. You don't want to be one of them.

*HC:* But if someone goes through a deep spiritual conversion, or repentance, or a turnaround, and sustains it for a significant amount of time, then you might consider trusting them again. But remember that lying is one of the most dangerous of all character problems, and without a significant reason for you to believe that some change has happened, you're really asking for trouble.

*JT:* Finally, if you don't want to be in relationship with a liar, be an honest person yourself. Be honest with yourself, first. It takes some self-deception to be with a liar for a long term, and if you're with one, you probably know some things about that person's character that you're not facing squarely. Don't lie to yourself.

*HC:* And stop lying to others. Be clear and honest about everything. That doesn't mean that you have to reveal all that you are thinking immediately. You don't have to talk about all of the feelings that you have or all of your intentions on the first date. You don't have to bring up every little offense. But in significant areas of life, you must not lie. You must not deceive. You have to be direct and clear.

*JT:* Be a person of the light, and the people of the light will then be drawn to you. And people of the darkness will not be able to tolerate the truth that you live. If you're an honest person, you will more likely end up with honest people. But if you deceive yourself or others, deceivers will be drawn to you. So be light and attract the light. And that's probably the best boundary of all.

# SESSION 3

## *Video Segment 1: "Right-Side-Up Dating"*

*Testimonial 1:* I always thought I was a pretty committed Christian—until I met Allen. He was such a great guy. He was respectful and considerate, thoughtful and generous. He had a great sense of humor, and he was so much fun to be around. Well, he wasn't "technically" committed to Christ, but I thought that would change. After all, I was pretty open about my faith—in the beginning. And then...I don't know...I guess I got embarrassed and shy about my faith. I don't know. I don't really know what happened, but I can see now that I was trying to fit my spiritual life into my dating life when my date didn't want God involved. I wasn't seeking to fit my dating life into my spiritual life, with what I knew God wanted me to do.

*Testimonial 2:* Meeting Bridget was the best thing that's ever happened to me. Her faith fueled mine, and we were on fire for the Lord. Then her cousin died unexpectedly. She starting asking all those questions like: "Why do bad things happen if God is all good and all powerful?" "Why does he allow suffering in the world?" I didn't know how to answer those questions. I mean, I couldn't just open my Bible and find them there either. I couldn't pray with her anymore because Bridget was just too angry at God to want to talk to him. She stopped going to worship because she didn't want people to ask her how she was doing. So there I was: not reading my Bible, not praying, not worshiping because Bridget wasn't either.

*Testimonial 3:* I'd always thought that I was pretty strong in my faith, until I met Todd. He has taught me so much! He's really helped me think through some of the tough issues of the faith. In fact, some of our best dates have been wrestling with these theological issues that I had never even considered. Don't get me wrong, Todd's faith isn't just an intellectual exercise. He truly loves the Lord, and he lives every day of his life expecting to see God work in very specific ways. And that's been good for me, too. Now I'm much more aware of God's presence with me and his goodness to me.

*JT:* Well, you've just heard from three people who've had varying degrees of success in taking God on a date, or more specifically, into a dating relationship. Now the first woman failed: She herself said, "I was trying to fit my spiritual life into my dating life. I wasn't seeking to having my dating life fit into my spiritual life, with what I knew God wanted me to do." That's upside-down dating. The issue needs to be how to fit our dating life into our spiritual life, not vice versa. Life and love are gifts of God, and they fall under his domain. So the right-side-up approach is to bring dating before God and ask for his guidance. It's good to offer our dating as part of the living sacrifice that helps submit all aspects of our lives to God's order for our own existence. The more our lives are surrendered to his ways, then the more he's able to fashion our lives as they were meant to be.

*HC:* We also heard from the guy who was dating Bridget. He seems to have started out strong. Christ was very much a part of what he and Bridget did and shared. But he soon found his own relationship with God changing depending on how Bridget was doing with God. He was excited about God when Bridget was doing well in her spiritual life, but he distanced himself from the Lord and didn't take responsibility for his spiritual health or growth when Bridget was working through the aftermath of her cousin's death. He wasn't owning his relationship with God for himself. Now, this kind of dependence on his date for the status of his relationship with God is really a form of idolatry.

By the way, when we demand that dating bring us the love, fulfillment, or desire we want without allowing God to point the way, we can miss God's design for us, and we run the risk of going to the creation, rather than the Creator, as our ultimate source of life. Many times people will find their relationship with God taking some sort of detour as their dating life becomes more involved. Again, surrendering all of your life to God is the first and necessary step of bringing dating in line with God.

*JT:* The third person we heard from did the best job of dating right-side-up. She had found a person who challenged her spiritually. She wasn't always being the instigator. She didn't have to provide the impetus for spiritual connection and growth. And that's one of six things to look for as a way for you to evaluate the fruit of your dating relationship, to consider whether your dating relationship brings you closer to God or pushes you further away him.

*HC:* Here are the six questions for you to ask yourself about your date.

- Does the person you date challenge you spiritually, rather than you having to be the impetus?
- Do you experience spiritual growth from interacting with that person?
- Are you drawn to God through that person?
- Do you have a connection with the other person in your spiritual life?
- Is the spiritual connection based on reality? Is the person real and authentic as well as spiritual?
- Is the relationship a place of mutual vulnerability about weaknesses, failures, or sins?

*JT:* Let's assume you're a committed Christian, and you're having a great time dating another Christian. Well now, you can share deeper parts of yourself and grow closer to each other and to God. Some of those deeper parts of yourself that you'll want to bring into your dating relationship are things like your faith journey, your values, your struggles, and all of the things that you learned spiritually, your friendships. Before you take some time to consider those aspects of your spiritual life, let me just say it's a great experience to be able to unveil yourself to your date spiritually as well as emotionally.

## Video Segment 2: "Walking Your Talk"

*HC:* We want to give you a few more thoughts about taking God on a date. First, let me remind you that differences can promote growth. Demanding that your date have exactly the same spiritual values as you could be a problem. You need to be in agreement on the fundamentals of your faith, but you also want to be in relationship with someone who has thought through their own spiritual issues deeply and individually, and has reached his or her own conclusions. So don't interpret religious agreement or even passivity on your date's part as something like compatibility. In fact, we'll encourage you to fall in love with someone who is passionate about matters of faith enough to wrestle with and discuss their meanings with you. Some of the most meaningful times of growth for dates can be when they argue, read the Bible, and come to terms on spiritual matters.

*JT:* Second, watch to see how your date integrates faith into real life. After all, there are religious people, and there are spiritual people. Religious people know the truth, but spiritual people do the truth. You want yourself and your date to have lives that reflect both knowing and doing spirituality in the real world. And that is what character is really all about. It's about integrating the realities of God's ways into everyday life and in all aspects of your life: the relational part, the financial part, the sexual part, the job part, and everything else that comprises life.

*HC:* Another aspect of the spiritual part of dating is that it is important to matter to each other on a spiritual level. Be part of each other's spiritual growth and conduct. Even if you don't end up marrying the person, you need to take the stance that during your tenure as dates, you both will grow spiritually. We encourage you to develop a relationship in which you're both challenging each other to "walk your talk." And evidence of walking your talk is found in two things: the ability to love and the ability to be humble. Truly spiritual people know they don't "have it all together." In fact, the opposite is true: they know how deep their failings are and how much they need God's grace and his love. And as a result, they're able to empty themselves and to love other people.

*JT:* Ultimately, the spiritual part of dating means we're to set limits on all sorts of desires and impulses within ourselves. We don't demand the other person to be compatible spiritually if they're not. We don't try to change the other person spiritually. We don't deny spiritual conflicts in the relationship. We don't overlook our own spiritual weaknesses and focus on our partner's. And we aren't afraid to address spiritual issues. However, as we continue to grow spiritually, it becomes easier to do these things. It becomes easier to love and invest our hearts wisely and well in our dating lives.

# SESSION 4

## *Video Segment 1: "A Boundary around Your Wish for Relationship"*

*Marsha:* Well, I finally did what I knew to be the right thing. I called him up and told him that it was over. I told him that I was tired of being hurt again and again and again, and that the pattern was always the same and I had no reason to believe that he was going to change. When I hung up, I was sad, you know, but there was some peace to it—until I heard him banging on my door. He said that he would never hurt me again, that he had learned his lesson, that he would even get counseling. But I held my ground, and eventually he left. Again, I was sad, but this time the relief was even greater.

But that was three days ago. And yesterday Scott and I got back together. I know, I know. I mean maybe it wasn't the wisest decision to make, but…I don't know… I just couldn't handle being alone.

*HC:* No one who knew Marsha would have suspected this agony she was going through. She was a strong person in the business world; she was a committed Christian and a leader in her church. And everybody loved her, and no one would have thought she would put up with somebody like Scott, or that she could be so devastated by breaking up with such a jerk. But breaking up with Scott was bringing out a deep aloneness that normally she did not even experience or know was there. And her history showed us that she avoided that aloneness by dating. She just couldn't stand to be alone. And her fear of being alone kept her from having boundaries with bad relationships. In fact, she would rather have a bad relationship than no relationship at all.

*JT:* Are you like Marsha? Are you giving up healthy boundaries because of a fear of aloneness? Well, here are some signs to tell:

1. Putting up with behavior that's disrespectful
2. Giving in to things that are not in accord with your own values
3. Settling for less than you know that you really desire or that you need
4. Staying in a relationship that you know has passed its deadline
5. Going back into a relationship that you know should be over
6. Getting into a relationship that you know is not going anywhere
7. Smothering the person that you're dating with excessive needs or control

*HC:* Surely there are other signs of the fear of being alone. But the point is, your dating is ruled by your internal isolation, rather than by your God, your goals, your values, and your spiritual commitments. Your aloneness makes you get involved in relationships that you know are not going to last. It also keeps you from being alone long enough to grow into a person who does not have to be in a relationship in order to be happy. There is a very important rule in dating and romance. Here it is: To be happy in a relationship, and to pick the kind of relationship that is going to be the kind you desire, you must be able to be happy without one.

*JT:* If you must be dating or married in order to be happy, you're dealing with what we call a dependency issue, and you'll never be happy with whatever person you find. And that dependency problem will keep you from being selective enough to find the right kind of person who'll be good for you. It'll also keep you from being able to fully realize a good relationship with a healthy person. So aloneness must be dealt with first, and this is a good boundary for dating. Here is the boundary: In order to cure your fear of being alone, put a boundary around your wish for a relationship. Deal with the nature of that wish and the fears that you have. Cure that fear first, and then go find a relationship.

## *Video Segment 2: "A Boundary with Your Past"*

*JT:* In researching this book, I interviewed married as well as single people to get their perspectives on the dating game. And one question I asked married people was, "Now that you're done with dating (we hope), what would you have done differently during those days?"

Here are some answers I received:

"I would've dated more people and not gotten so heavily involved in that one relationship."

"I would've been more honest about myself and my values."

"I would've developed more real friendships and less of these intense dating relationships."

"I would've gotten a life instead of spending so much time and energy dating."

"I would've learned more from my previous mistakes."

*JT:* The majority of responses were like that last person's, and I think his or her answer means, "If I could've done things differently, I would've done things differently." People wish they could've benefited more from their experiences. In fact, the statements we just heard can help you begin to evaluate your dating past. Did you date too seriously? Was it difficult for you to be honest? Did you neglect your friendships? Did your life revolve around dating instead of your dating being part of a balanced life? When you recognize patterns like these, you can begin to work through them.

*HC:* It's important to set a boundary with your past, that is, to deal with your old dating patterns as something that you're not destined to continue. You know, your past can be your best friend or your worst enemy in terms of helping you develop the right sort of dating relationships.

*JT:* You know, the past is important because it's the repository of all of your trial-and-error experiences. Your past can provide a great deal of necessary information on what to do and what to avoid in dating, either through the satisfaction that you did it right or the pain that you did it wrong. And to just skip over the past is to ignore some very important aspects of reality. Pay attention to what you've done, and you'll take ownership of your present and your future.

*HC:* Your past affects your dating. So don't neglect your past just because your present is good. And work on making your past work for you instead of against you. Key to that is becoming a good historian of yourself.

*JT:* Let me give you an example. I have a friend who's been praying a lot for several years to find a husband. She's pretty frustrated with the failures of her relationships. But when I asked her recently what she thought the problem was, she said, "Well, the guys just aren't the right guys." Well, until my friend sees that she is the common denominator in all these "bad" guys, I don't see how things are going to change. In fact, the first dating problem is denying that your past demonstrates a problem.

*HC:* So if you tend to get with your buddies or girlfriends and have gripe sessions about the lack of quality dating material in the world, do something constructive. Ask them, God, and yourself the same question: What can I learn from my dating past that will help me avoid bad things or experience good things in the future? Now this requires a lot more work than griping does, and is nowhere nearly as enjoyable, but it does tend to produce good results. An even more pointed question is this: What have I done to contribute to my dating problems today? This isn't about condemning yourself or being on your case. Instead, it's about a quest for truth and reality to free you from repeating the same mistakes over and over again. It's about setting and maintaining a healthy boundary with your past.

# SESSION 5

## *Video Segment 1: "What You Can—and Can't—Live With"*

*HC:* I bet you have in mind just the kind of person you want to date or marry. If I asked you, "What do you look for in a person that you want to date seriously or marry?" you could probably list a few things without any hesitation. And your answers might be something like these. Watch.

> *Interviewer:* What do you look for in a person to date seriously or marry?
> *Person 1:* Well, I need to see a deep spiritual commitment to God.
> *Person 2:* A real love for God's Word.
> *Person 3:* Someone with ambition and goals.
> *Person 4:* Someone who's fun to be with.
> *Person 5:* A guy [or girl] with lots of enthusiasm for life.
> *Person 6:* I think a person who's attractive both outwardly and inwardly.
> *Person 7:* Someone who's smart, who thinks.
> *Person 8:* It's gotta be someone who likes sports.
> *Person 9:* Someone who's a leader in their field, and someone who succeeds at what they set out to do.
> *Person 10:* I want someone who can make me laugh.

*HC:* Great list, isn't it? But you know, in all the years of marriage counseling I've done, I have yet to meet a couple who was ready to split up or having significant problems because one was not witty enough, or didn't read the Bible as much as the other wished, or was not a leader in their field.

*JT:* The traits the people just mentioned are differences in taste. Some people want athletic people, and others want the intellectual type. Well, differences like these, they make the world go round. But certain traits have nothing to do with tastes and natural differences. These traits are to be avoided if you're thinking of getting into a serious dating relationship or one which might head to marriage. These traits have to do with character.

*HC:* As I told one young woman, "You're initially attracted to somebody's outsides, but over time you'll experience their insides." That's what character is all about. The person's character is what you will experience long-term in the relationship. So, as you consider the character of the person you want to date, we want you to look at your "boundaries of choices." We want you to look at what your requirements are for the people that you date. If you know ahead of time what you will not put up with in a dating relationship, you could save yourself from a season or even a lifetime of misery. Now, on the other hand you might be a little too rigid in your preferences and closing yourself off to some really good people.

*JT:* There are basically four areas that you need to examine.

First, are your preferences too limiting? Do you need to be a little more open?

Secondly, are some preferences more important than you realize? You need to value those.

Third, which imperfections in a person's character are just minor? You'll need to learn to deal with them.

Fourth, which imperfections in a person's character are major? These are totally off-limits. You should not ever have to live with them.

*HC:* It's that last point we want to say more about. Keep in mind that, because of the very nature of human beings, relationships will be imperfect—every one of them. You're always going to be dating somebody with flaws. But remember, there are flaws that you can live with and flaws you really can't live with. And the ones that you can live with can teach you a lot about things like patience and acceptance and being a loving person, as well as intimacy and how to work through conflict. But serious character flaws can injure or even destroy you. The best test is God's Word, and how your own heart feels as you are with that person in the relationship. What does it feel like to be with them over time?

*JT:* If you are dealing with a person who injures you, leaves you feeling bad about yourself and love, and hurts you in other ways, you're dealing with things that you shouldn't be allowing. The best test is always your own experience of that person. Protect yourself by knowing what you feel and what you value, and have the courage to stick to what you value for your dating life. Ultimately, we always get what we value. So value good things, and say no to things that destroy.

*HC:* Finally, in the shallow area of preferences—like physical appearance, personality types, and other kinds—we suggest you be open to casually dating anybody of good character as long as they're not dangerous. You might find out a lot about yourself and also have a lot of fun. Dating's a time to get to know people and to learn about life, and you, and the world, and how other people are. If the person is of good character, go out and have a good time.

# Video Segment 2: "Beware When Opposites Attract"

*Interviewer:* Tell me a little bit about your relationship with your boyfriend.
*Person 1:* Well, he's good at making money, and I'm good at spending it.
*Person 2:* He's really strong, and I'm pretty insecure.
*Person 3:* Well, you know, she's like a people person, and I'm kinda into my own space and all that.
*Person 4:* Well, she's confident, but I need reassurance.
*Person 5:* He makes up for what I'm not in a way, and I'd say he completes me.

*JT:* The idea of complementary gifts and strengths is really good for us emotionally and in many ways. We have to learn humility to ask people for what we don't have and that helps us grow. For example, if your date is really perceptive in relationships, you might ask him why you're struggling in your relationship with your roommate. We can also grow from the competencies of other people.

*HC:* We should use and appreciate the abilities of those who have what we don't. However, the danger occurs when we make opposing styles or abilities the basis for a relationship. At the outset, it might seem like a good thing. You're complementing each other. You provide what the other one needs. You're stimulated by the other's different point of view. It seems all good.

*JT:* But the danger of going for an opposite-type person, however, is this: Opposite-driven relationships often confuse dependency with love. That is, people may feel intense longings for an "opposite" person, and they may appreciate the "completion" that they feel with that person. But they run the risk of simply needing that person for those particular functions, and it never gives the true loving feelings in relationships that they need to grow and flourish. Dependency is just a part of love. It's not the full expression of love. The full expression of love is to give it back from a full heart.

*HC:* In our experience, the degree of attraction that opposites have for each other is often diagnostic of the couple's maturity. You see, in mature couples, opposite traits are simply not a major issue. They don't fight about them; they quarrel about them. The two people aren't even drawn to opposite traits due to their own deficits. They're drawn to the values they share, such as love, responsibility, forgiveness, honesty, and their spirituality. Attraction based on values is much more mature than just the attraction based on what you don't possess inside of yourself.

*JT:* On the other hand, immature couples seem to struggle more with finding someone who possesses the nurturance, or the structure, or the competence, or the personality that they don't have. Ultimately, they're looking for a parent to take care of part of them that they can't take care of themselves.

*HC:* So make opposites a nonissue. Look more for character, for love, and for values than "who has what." Don't fall for an introvert just because you are an extrovert. Fall for someone who calls you into love, growth, and God. And then appreciate the unique differences between the two of you.

# SESSION 6

## *Video Segment 1: "Don't Fall in Love with Someone You Wouldn't Be Friends With"*

*Sam:* Stephanie and I are really good friends. But whatever that "thing" is that attracts you to someone—that "falling in love" thing—I just don't have it with Stephanie. But Kimberly—now there's someone who's easy to fall in love with. That "falling in love" thing—it was there from the start. But while she's easy to fall in love with, I'm not sure I'd feel really comfortable with her in the long run. There's not a whole lot between us—of substance, you know? Like with Stephanie.

*HC:* It sounds to me like Sam thinks he's in love with Kim, but he has more of a real relationship with Stephanie. After all, she's the one who really connects with him. She's the one who has an ability to share things that matter, to communicate, to have fun with Sam. But on the other hand, he enjoys the sparks and the chemistry with Kim. But maybe Sam is letting his relationship with Kim blind him to some very important things that are essential for a good, lasting relationship. In short, he might be falling in love with a woman that he would not choose as a friend.

*JT:* Many singles we've known share Sam's problem, and perhaps you do, too. Maybe you simply find that the person you're attracted to is not able to connect with all areas of your life. But in other cases, you're attracted to someone who is not good for you at all. You may have all sorts of longings and chemistry with someone who's not only lacking some abilities but who also has some pretty destructive things going on about her character.

*HC:* Here's what we tell singles who have this problem of, as we put it, falling in love with someone they wouldn't be friends with. First, if you're attracted to someone who does not possess the character and the friendship qualities that you need in a long-term relationship, don't think you're going to change him or her.

*JT:* Second, if this is your pattern, see it as a problem, not simply a matter of "I haven't found the 'right one' yet."

*HC:* Third, do everything possible to get to know the person that you're attracted to: Can you share all of your values? Is the spiritual commitment the same? Are there character traits that you find yourself ignoring, denying, or even making excuses for? In short, would you pick this person that you're attracted to as a friend?

*JT:* Are you confusing longing or desire for "being in love"? Many times people desire a certain kind of fantasy person, and they think that this deep longing is being in love when it's not.

*HC:* Are you confusing infatuation with love? Remember that phrase "in fat you ate." Well, infatuation's similar to a lot of that high-fat fast food. There's really no lasting nutritional value for your soul.

*JT:* Finally, and most importantly, find an accountability system to hold you to the boundary of not letting yourself go too far into a relationship with someone that you just can't be friends with. Say no to letting your heart get involved with a person that you wouldn't choose as a friend.

*HC:* The best boundary that you can have in your dating life is to begin every relationship with an eye towards friendship.

## *Video Segment 2: "Don't Ruin a Friendship out of Loneliness"*

*Ted:* Ellen and I went to the wedding and, yeah, it was tough. Because people looked at us and—well you know how they are at weddings: they're looking for the next subjects. They're putting people together, wondering, "Now why don't they date?" Well, they asked that about Ellen and me.

*Ellen:* Ted and I have been best friends since junior high school. But we really hit it off in that science class with Mr. LeMay. We've been best friends ever since. I'm sure people think we'll get together.

*Ted:* "You two seem really right for each other. Why don't you date? Go beyond the friendship thing."

*Ellen:* Well, why not?

*Ted:* So we did. . .and—

*Ellen:* It was. . .it was like. . .

*Ted:* Kissing your sister!

*Ellen:* Yeah, we decided what we've both known the whole time: We are much better as friends than as dates.

*Ted:* Oh, yeah.

*Ellen:* Much better. Yeah.

*HC:* Ted and Ellen's friendship is an example of two things. First, it illustrates how much good can come from healthy opposite-sex relationships. And second, it shows how much grief they spared themselves by not pursuing a romantic relationship when the necessary things weren't there.

*JT:* In this part of the session, we want to help you experience the good that comes from friendships and avoid the problems that come from making friends into something that they're really not.

*HC:* "Romanticizing a friendship" is the phrase we use to refer to as making friends into something they're not. Romantic feelings come from an idealization of the other person. This idealization can be caused by several things, both healthy and unhealthy.

*JT:* In a new relationship, you don't know much about the other person. Idealization fills in those gaps with good things in order to keep the couple involved in the relationship, and helps them tolerate the early parts of the developing connection.

*HC:* In a mature relationship, romantic idealization waxes and wanes. It comes from a deep appreciation and gratitude for the person's presence and love, yet it retains the reality of who he or she is at the same time. Both of these things are normal.

*JT:* In a struggling relationship, one person can develop romantic feelings for the other out of his or her own neediness. And this neediness becomes "romanticized"; that is, it disguises its true nature of need in romance. The person feels alive, and driven, and motivated to be with the other. Yet the need is generally caused by an emptiness inside. This kind of romanticization can ruin a perfectly good friendship and is driven by loneliness.

*HC:* And we don't mean the loneliness that comes for a salesman on a long business trip who feels lonely for his support network while he's out on the road and then takes steps to reconnect when he returns. We're talking about the condition—the condition that goes on and on—of loneliness that's a problem inside of a person. This type of loneliness is a chronic, longstanding sense of emptiness in life, no matter what the circumstances. The person can be around many loving, caring people, and still feel isolated. She may either feel that others don't care or that she's unable to receive what they give. This loneliness is an indication that something is broken in one's soul and needs to be repaired in God's healing process, not by a friendship-turned-romantic.

# SESSION 7

## *Video Segment 1: "Adapt Now, Pay Later"*

*Keri:* He got really angry the other day when I told him I had to take a trip to cover a story for a client. He said he didn't want me to go. He told me—and he wasn't very gentle—"This just doesn't work for me. You have to make a choice. It's either your work or me." And then he drove off…and he's right, Sandy. I mean, I just can't expect to have my own career and to make somebody happy at the same time. I'm just going to have to find another way to work. I just hope I haven't lost him.

*Sandy:* Wait a minute. You're wrong in thinking that you can't have your career and relationship, too.

*Keri:* I know, I mean, but maybe I can work less…or I can be more selective about traveling…

*Sandy:* Keri! Listen to yourself. This is hard to say, but I would want you to tell me if you saw something going on in my life. It seems to me that Steve likes you, but only when you're doing what he likes. Think about it: He's making all the choices, all the plans. He's affecting your work, and your friendships, too. He's taking charge. No, he's taking over. Has he ever adapted himself to doing what you want to do? I think you need to stand your ground and find out what kind of person he really is. And he needs to find out who you really are!

*JT:* The truth that Sandy spoke in love was hard for Keri to hear. But Sandy helped her see that she had not been herself with Steve. Keri realized that as long as she adapted to Steve and his wishes and his wants, things went very well. But as soon as she began to be a real person with needs and desires of her own, he was unable to deal with the equality. It was his way or the highway.

*HC:* Sandy took a risk when she was honest with Keri, but Sandy also helped Keri avoid a train wreck. Better to find out early in a relationship that you are with someone who cannot adapt to your wishes than to find out much later or, God forbid, after marriage.

*JT:* Keri was grateful for Sandy's honesty, and she learned an important lesson: Don't be someone you're not just to gain that person's love. If you do, the person that your loved one is loving is not you. It is the role that you're playing and it's not your true self who is being loved.

*HC:* You're a person, and you cannot go through life without pursuing your own wishes, and needs, and desires—nor should you have to. Your needs and desires are going to come out, and you'd better find out early in the relationship how the person you're dating will sometimes have to adapt to you as well.

*JT:* The first lesson in this session is to be yourself from the beginning. If you're a real person from the start, a relationship of mutuality does have a chance of developing. If you're not, then you might be headed for trouble.

# *Video Segment 2: "Too Much, Too Fast"*

*JT:* One of my closest friends is a talented songwriter. When we were college buddies, I visited him in his room one day. He picks up his guitar and says, "Wanna hear my new love song?" I said I did, and he sang this song, "I love you. Always have, always will. What's your name?"

*HC:* Those song lyrics reflect the topic of this video: too much, too fast. The problem of premature commitment and overinvolvement in dating relationships is a common one. Two people find they have strong feelings for each other, and they quickly begin investing enormous amounts of time in the relationship. They neglect other people; they neglect their interests and activities. The couple is typified by a drivenness to become highly committed quickly, a process that takes less than a normal amount of time.

*JT:* What's normal? Well, the Bible's not explicit about this, but we would suggest that a year, not including the engagement period, is a pretty good minimum. When you date for at least a year, you experience the rhythm of life and a wide variety of experiences, including holidays, fiscal financial periods, vacations, school terms, and all that. You can see how the relationship weathers the flow of both people's lives.

*HC:* Yet many people meet, date, and mate within a few months or even weeks. They believe they've recognized the right person and think they're ready for marriage. Or some couples will take the needed year or two to date, but will have a problem in "frontloading" the relationship: They've become committed very soon in the game, and never go through a process of gradually becoming closer over time. Couples like these see time as the enemy. And what contributes to this? Well, we'll talk about four of the many reasons that do.

*JT:* First, loneliness. Loneliness is one of the most painful yet necessary experiences in human life. People feel incomplete, empty, or even starving inside. Loneliness can make us do almost anything to fill up the hole inside. So some of us rush a relationship. Don't do that. Instead, use your loneliness as a signal—a signal to get connected with some good, solid, nondating relationships.

*HC:* Second, some couples "couple" too quickly because they haven't finished the task of emotionally leaving home. They're unable to navigate the single adult life. They don't enjoy it, and they're still emotionally dependent on their family of origin, and so at some level they're yearning for a home environment that they never finished leaving. So they opt more for the marriage state than really opting for the right person.

*JT:* Third, some people overcommit due to problems in making deep and lasting friendships. They find it hard to get truly close to people, and instead of developing a good community, they choose one romantic relationship to focus on.

*HC:* And then fourth, perfectionism can cause people to commit too quickly. You might think that, being too picky, perfectionists would never marry. But some perfectionists become quickly committed to a person who represents every weakness they don't have. Their friends will scratch their heads in bewilderment. But that person, being unable to resolve his or her own weaknesses, their badness, or their imperfections, falls in love with someone who possesses all of those things. She's still in relationship with all parts of herself, but she doesn't have to take ownership or responsibility for them.

*HC:* If your dating relationships tend to move too quickly, consider that a signal and ask yourself why. Make sure that you're not moving quickly because you're avoiding some other pain, such as loneliness or some kind of inner hurt that you need to resolve.

*JT:* Quick and intense relationships often end up either burning out or being pretty shallow. Real love takes time. It doesn't have a shortcut, but it's worth it. Ask God to make you patient with the process of love so you'll be able to experience its growth day by day.

# SESSION 8

## *Video Segment 1: "Don't Get Kidnapped"*

*Debbie:* I thought I'd learned some things when I broke off the engagement. I got back in touch with my friends. I was involved in church activities and loving my times with the Lord. I was learning to sail and taking classes at the local art studio. I was going out with two or three different guys and really enjoying being with my friends. And volunteering at the shelter for abused women was the best! I was on a pretty good program—and thanking God for helping me get there.

Then I met Nick. We hit it off right away and began spending a lot of time together. Soon he was the only guy I was dating and, in fact, the only person I was really spending any time with at all.

I did miss my friends, but they were excited that I was happy with Nick. I just wished though that Nick had been more excited about meeting them and hanging out with them. But he wasn't, so I spent a lot of time on the beach, catching up on reading while Nick surfed. He didn't want to do any of the things that I was interested in, but I thought I couldn't have it all. I'd also realized that he didn't have any interest in going to church or doing a Bible study with me, but I figured that would happen eventually as he continued to grow in the Lord. But Nick didn't change at all.

*HC:* Debbie had been kidnapped. She should have had time, space, friends, and interests alone, apart from Nick. And vice versa. Her friends would have been part of this separateness that would provide space and freedom from Nick, even if the relationship had been going well. A relationship that gets rid of one's individual life and friends and time and space completely is not a healthy relationship. Your friends are an important space-giving freedom that will help you to be healthier and more well-rounded in your relationship. In addition, they will notice if you're losing them to some dating relationship, and they can tell you.

*JT:* Work out your dating relationship with the help of your friends. Spend time and energy with your dates, but then return to your community. This especially becomes important if you have some strong stance to take in time of conflict or change. Call a friend to give you courage and call them back to be accountable.

*HC:* And don't even attempt to get serious in a dating relationship until you're connected to a good support system and friends who really know you. If you are what we call "dating in a vacuum," you're in a lot of danger. Then, stay involved with your friends and community as an individual while you're dating.

*JT:* One aspect of "safe dating" is to remain connected to your friends and your support system. Make sure that you're not vulnerable to what you cannot see, but with the help of other people would otherwise be able to see very clearly. Stay connected, stay safe, and stay wise.

## *Video Segment 2: "Boundaries on Blame"*

*Person 1:* Why do you always...?
*Person 2:* I can't believe you've done it again.
*Person 3:* You're so...
*Person 4:* I don't deserve this kind of treatment.
*Person 5:* This is all your fault.
*Person 6:* Who do you think you are?
*Person 7:* After all I've done for you...

*JT:* If you have a habit of saying these or similar statements to your date, you're not alone. To some extent, blame is part of the human condition; you come by it honestly. Adam and Eve modeled and passed that trait down through the generations. They pointed the finger of blame on the devil, each other, and even God.

*HC:* What is blaming? Blaming is ascribing responsibility to someone for a fault. When we accuse another of a problem, we're blaming. Blame is not bad in and of itself. It has a good function. Blame separates out who is truly responsible for what in any given problem, so that we're able to know how to solve it. Blame helps differentiate what is our fault, and what's another's.

*JT:* For example, your girlfriend invited you to a party. She was vague about whether or not her ex would be there. But you also gave the impression that it wouldn't bother you, which wasn't true. So you go and you have this miserable time at the party. And, as you blame, you figure out that she was at fault for not being clear, and you were at fault for not being honest about your feelings. You both know what your growth tasks are to resolve this kind of issue. Blame really did help point the way to the solutions.

*HC:* However, the blame that kills a good dating relationship is when one person sees herself as blameless and attributes almost all the problems in the relationship to the other person. This sort of blame is not driven by any kind of a desire to figure out whose fault it is or in order to come to some truth about the matter. This type of blame is the blame that's based on denial of our own self. When we can't tolerate the reality of our own mistakes, or others might see that reality, then we point the finger somewhere else. And that ends up in our really being out of control of our dating and our lives.

*JT:* Blame is one of the gravest problems that we face spiritually and emotionally. It keeps us more concerned about being "good" than about being honest. The best thing you can do for yourself spiritually, as well as in your dating life, is to begin learning to accept blame for what is truly yours and to give up blaming for what is not another's fault.

*HC:* For several reasons, however, dating—by its very nature—is a really fertile place for blame to grow. First, the relationship may not be permanent, and blaming is an easier solution than seeing your part in triggering someone's faults and working on your own character development. Second, you may struggle with blame just as some people struggle with selfishness, or impulsiveness, or passivity. And your tendency to blame may emerge more in the dating arena. Finally, the romance of dating can be emotional and it can be intense. This intensity can tap into old needs and desires from when we were even children. During the low part of the childlike swings, blame can take hold, just like a two-year-old blames everyone else. People who have unresolved hurts in childhood issues may unwittingly blame their date for things the other person isn't even guilty of.

*JT:* So what can you do about our tendency to blame? Well, first, learn to humbly listen to correction and restrain the urge to react in blame. Secondly, let the blame signal you to see if you're afraid, or you're scared or feel judged, or if you're just really sad about some fault you have. Third, take a strong stance of being more concerned about your soul's state than that of your date's. And then next, accept what is really negative about your date and work with the realities instead of staying locked in a protest stance of arguing and blaming. Also, ask those you trust to let you know when you play the blame game. And finally, learn to be a forgiver—and make mutual forgiveness a part of your dating relationships.

# SESSION 9

## *Video Segment 1: "Say No to Disrespect"*

*Craig:* It was our first date at a fancy restaurant. I tried to go all out and make it a nice, romantic evening. Anyway, the waiter comes by, you know the beach-type, good looking. "Hi, I'm Josh, and I'll be your server tonight. Can I get you anything to start off?" And Cindy goes, "Sure, Josh, if you're on the menu." Then they both laugh. I was in shock. I mean, this was a side of her I'd never seen before, and it blew me away. It was also kind of embarrassing. So after Josh left I told her that what she said really bothered me. She said that she was just making a joke and that I was overreacting.

But then a week after that, we were at a party. My friend told Cindy and I that his girlfriend had just broken up with him. And Cindy goes, "She must be nuts. If I had someone with your looks and personality, I'd be thanking my lucky stars." I don't know, but I'm not feeling a whole lot of respect here.

*JT:* Disrespect is a serious obstacle to closeness, intimacy, and even a couple's chances for marital success. Every person needs to feel like the person they're getting to know respects them. And what is respect? It's the ability to value another person's experience. Empathy is the ability to feel another person's experience, especially the painful ones. Now you may not be able to actually empathize with someone always, but you can always take a position of respect for them.

*HC:* When respect is present, the other person feels that he can be free to be who he is. He still can be honest, still feel connected and feel safe. He doesn't worry that he's going to be attacked, humiliated, or treated poorly. When respect is absent though, many people will find themselves controlled, or neglected, or injured by someone who doesn't care about their needs or feelings.

*JT:* A disrespectful relationship ultimately has to do with character. Selfishness, control, lack of understanding, all sorts of other things can cause disrespect. Keep in mind that if someone is genuinely trying to change his disrespectful ways, it is not disrespectful to fail. However, it's disrespectful to continually fail in an area that hurts another and to not take any steps to resolve that problem.

*HC:* So respect and esteem your date's thoughts, feelings, and choices—and require that same sort of treatment from him or her. And address early in the relationship any disrespect that you notice. If you feel disrespected and you aren't really sure it's really going on, ask your date and get the dialogue started. Also, don't fight fire with fire. Start with vulnerability and state your desire for the relationship to be better.

*JT:* Two more points. First, see if you're making it easier to be disrespected by putting yourself in the one-down position in the relationship. And, finally, make a distinction between differences and disrespect. You can disagree and you can even get angry with each other respectfully.

## Video Segment 2: "Set Up a Detention Hall"

*JT:* For the next few minutes, we want to talk about solving problems of love, respect, responsibility, and commitment in dating relationships. Though no one has the power to fix anyone else, you do have the power to respond in healthy ways with your date when problems arise. And healthy responses, which often involve the careful and caring use of boundaries, can really go a long way toward a better relationship.

*HC:* There are healthy ways to deal with a dating relationship in which there are boundary violations going on. One person is losing freedom and love, and one person is "playing and not paying." We'll be addressing the "boundary bustee," the one that's getting violated, rather than the "boundary buster" because the one who's reaping what someone else is sowing is typically more motivated to do something about the problem.

*JT:* First of all, realize that some conflict is normal. Problems, including boundary conflicts, are just a normal part of relationships. So give up the demand that your relationship be conflict-free. It won't happen. Get over it, and go the next step.

*HC:* And that step is to require boundaries in your relationship. Don't wait to set a limit until there's some huge problem or crisis in your love life. Boundaries should be woven into the fabric of your life and relationships—all of them, every day—as something that you do and say routinely. Setting limits is simply about being honest about what you allow and what you don't allow. Make honesty, responsibility, respect, and freedom a required part of all aspects of your relationships: socially, emotionally, sexually, spiritually, and in every other area of life.

*JT:* If that sounds scary, deal with your fear of setting limits. Begin to see boundaries as a tool for diagnosing the character of your date and of the relationship. Basically, think about boundaries as preserving the relationship, rather than ending it.

*HC:* Once you see the problem, then approach your date from a stance of love and respect, and mutuality or equality. Your best approach is to be very specific with your date about the boundary problem. Have specific events that you can draw from to show your point and show what you felt like really happened, and what was the real problem with what was going on. Also talk about what you wished would have happened instead—the way you really like for things to go.

*JT:* A few words now about setting boundaries. When you set boundaries, you are allowing pain—the pain of consequences for their actions—to touch someone important to you. The conflict of wanting the closeness, and yet having to take a righteous stance with a boundaryless person, can really take its toll. We've identified seven things to have in place as you go through the boundary-setting process.

1. Stay connected.
2. Avoid the reactive friend.
3. Expect negative reactions from your date.
4. Empathize with the struggle.
5. Be patient.
6. Question motives.
7. And provide a way back to normal relationships.

These terms are defined in your notes.

# Session 10

## *Video Segment 1: "The Big Rule—and Why"*

*Jenny:* Dave and I had been dating for a while. We spent a lot of time together, doing things that we both enjoyed, you know, from Bible studies and movies, to sports and reading. And I felt like I was falling in love.

And there was nothing like being in his arms. And our hugs turned into kisses and with those kisses our desire for each other just grew. And we were both committed to abstinence before marriage, and so we would always back off just in time...until one night.

And I don't know how my values got so far away...

But the next morning I felt awful. I had stood so strong and had been so committed, and I knew what God wanted for me. But I was guilty, and I felt guilty. I still feel guilty. I'm more in love with him now than ever. And, I mean, I just don't see how loving someone physically can be so wrong. You know, I mean...it was wonderful to be that close and...it felt right. But, I knew it was wrong.

*HC:* Okay, let's talk. Here is the issue: You're past thirteen, you're single, and you've got a body that is ready for sex. But you're not married. What do you do? How far is too far? Why should you wait? Are you missing out on something good for no reason? Or is there good reason to have limits on sexual expression? Besides, will he still love you if you say no? Or, if you really loved him, wouldn't you say yes? Questions like these are really good to ask.

*JT:* And the big answer to questions like these, the big rule so to speak, is that God wants people to reserve sex for marriage. But, for many people, both inside and outside of the church, it just doesn't make sense to them. But for those who have reaped the consequences of the pain that sex outside of marriage can bring, they know that there are good reasons to wait—and Dr. Cloud and I agree on this. We'll explain why.

*HC:* We'll start by looking at the rule, and it's found in 1 Thessalonians 4:3–8. "It is God's will that you should be sanctified: that you should avoid sexual immorality; that each of you should learn to control his own body in a way that is holy and honorable, not in passionate lust like the heathen, who do not know God; and that in this matter no one should wrong his brother or take advantage of him. The Lord will punish men for all such sins, as we have already told you and warned you. For God did not call us to be impure, but to live a holy life. Therefore [it goes on to say] he who rejects this instruction does not reject man but God, who gives you his Holy Spirit." Pretty tough rules.

*JT:* You may have noticed that the statement of the rule contains five reasons why God calls for sexual abstinence outside marriage. First, Paul calls God's people to "control [their] body in a way that is holy and honorable" (1 Thess. 4:4). Now what does that mean? *Holiness* means "purity." It means "being set aside for a high purpose." *Honor* means things like "dignity, precious, of high price or value, or high esteem." So, first, God's saying that sex is not a casual thing. Like other things of very high value, to spend sex casually or unwisely is foolish, and it will cheat you.

*HC:* Paul also says, "Each [one] of you should learn to control his own body" (1 Thess. 4:4). Control of one's body is a sign that, and get this, a person is capable of delay of gratification and has self-control. And here's why it's important: Those are prerequisites of the ability to truly love. That's reason number two why God reserves sex for marriage.

And reason number three is related. Paul teaches against something called "passionate lust" (1 Thess. 4:5), which is a lust for that which is forbidden outside of marriage. A healthy person is someone who is what we call "integrated." In other words, the body, the soul, and the mind are all working together. If someone hasn't married you, then they've given less than 100 percent of themselves and, therefore, they should get less than 100 percent of your body. Also, passionate lust does something that psychologists call "splits a person" from their real heart, their mind, and their values, and the life they truly desire. Lust gets momentary fulfillment, but it's at the expense of lasting gain.

*JT:* Next, reason number four. Paul also teaches that when sex occurs outside of marriage, someone is always wronged (1 Thess. 4:6). When someone sleeps with a person with whom he or she is not married, he or she is hurting that person. If you say that you're a person of love, then you won't wrong someone that you love. You'll wait. And vice versa, don't allow anyone else to wrong you. Love can wait to give; lust cannot wait to get.

And, finally, reason number five, Paul teaches us that the authority for sexuality really doesn't even belong to us; it belongs to God. There are few better tests for whether or not someone lives a life in submission to God than what he or she does with their sexuality. God wants to be accepted as he really is, rules and all. When someone rewrites God's values, they're not accepting who God really is; they're making him up. Be sure you're trusting a person who really trusts the God that is. Because if he or she is trusting God, that person will uphold God's value of sex within marriage.

*HC:* Let me add that it's difficult to keep someone out of your heart who's invaded your body. That in itself is another reason to say no to sex outside of marriage.

*JT:* Sexuality is a part of God's good creation; it's great. But, as you embrace your sexuality, you're going to need to do so with self-control, sanctity, high esteem, lovingly and not lustfully, sacrificially and not "wronging" someone, and in submission to God.

## Video Segment 2: "Critical Measures of a Good Dating Relationship"

*JT:* As this series draws to a close, we hope you haven't become too discouraged. Learning to have good boundaries in dating is work and it does take some time, but we really believe that it pays off. We also hope that you now understand how to better conduct your dating life to develop good things like love, freedom, and responsibility in both you and whomever you're dating.

*HC:* Boundaries in dating is about becoming a truthful, caring, responsible, and free person who encourages growth in those you are in contact with. There're several aspects to always be monitoring as you date. So, in closing, we'll look at six critical measures of a good dating relationship to help make sure that the good things that God has designed can actually occur in your dating life.

*JT:* First, is dating growing you up? Are you learning, for example, how to safely open up about your feelings, are you learning how to take risks, and make decisions with the person that you're dating? Are you learning about your own issues and about how you affect other people, and what to do about them?

*HC:* Second, is dating bringing you closer to God? Is your spiritual life deeper and more meaningful as a result of who you are and how you date?

*JT:* Third, are you more able to have good relationships? Is dating helping you to deepen your capacity for healthy intimacy, and increasing your ability to trust and depend on other people for your emotional needs? Is it growing you into a more loving and truthful person? If your dating life is making you withdraw from other people, or discourages you, or choose worse people? There's something wrong and it needs to be repaired.

*HC:* And then fourthly, are you picking better dates over time? Are you fine-tuning the types of people that you're becoming involved with? Are you able to identify those who fit who you are and who you want to be? In short, are you choosing people of more mature character?

*JT:* Fifth, are you a better potential mate? Kind of get rid of the idea that you're fine and you just gotta go find the "right person." That's crazy. Learn from your dating life how you might make a mate miserable. Are you selfish? Are you irresponsible? Are you detached? Are you emotionally inaccessible? Well, start to work on those things that would disqualify you from loving a mate deeply.

*HC:* Sixth, are you enjoying the ride? Even though it is important growth work, dating should be a lot of fun. You can have great times with good people as you work on healthy boundaries in dating. Now, if the bad times are more frequent than the good, evaluate or figure out what's going on. Dating well now can help ensure a loving, satisfying, and full marriage relationship when God brings you together with someone in that kind of bond.

*JT:* Finally, we do pray that God's hand will be on all your dating relationships and activities. God bless you in your own boundaries and dating.

For information on books, resources, or speaking engagements:

Cloud-Townsend Resources
3176 Pullman Avenue, Suite 104
Costa Mesa, CA 92626
Phone: 1-800-676-HOPE (4673)
Web: www.cloudtownsend.com

# About the Writer

Lisa Guest writes, edits, and develops curriculum from her home in Irvine, California, where she lives with her husband and two children. She has written two books, *Small Miracles* and *A Mother's Love*. She enjoys swimming, reading, and playing with her kids.

# How a Well-Timed "No" Can Triple the Joy of Saying "Yes"

## Boundaries

(Revised)

*When to Say Yes, When to Say No to Take Control of Your Life*

Dr. Henry Cloud & Dr. John Townsend
0-310-22362-8

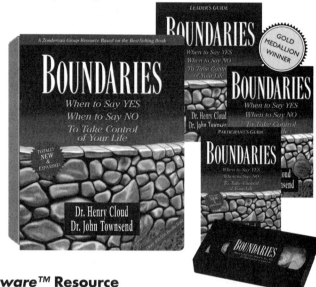

**A Zondervan*Groupware*™ Resource**
**Based on the Best-Selling Book**
—Totally new and expanded
—Over 400,000 books sold

Zondervan*Groupware*

*Do you have trouble saying no?* • **Can you set limits and still be a loving person?**
Are you in control of your life? • What are legitimate boundaries?
**Do people take advantage of you?**
*How do you answer someone who wants your time, love, energy, and money?*

Dr. Henry Cloud and Dr. John Townsend offer biblically based answers to these tough questions as they show us how to set healthy boundaries with our parents, our spouses, our children, our friends, our coworkers, and even ourselves. This compelling, nine-part video resource helps us define and maintain the clear personal boundaries that are essential to a healthy and balanced Christian life.

Applying the proven "group-interactive" format designed to enhance participation and learning among small-group members, *Boundaries* helps us discover the impact of boundaries on all areas of our lives.

It shows us:

- How to know where our responsibilities begin and end
- How to be free to choose the right things for ourselves in the light of God's will
- How to say no to irresponsible or controlling people
- How to say yes for the right reasons
- How to deal with guilt and the fear of losing love

With brief video dramatizations and discussion jump-starters by Drs. Cloud and Townsend, the *Boundaries* Zondervan*Groupware* resource provides everything needed to successfully conduct nine lively, life-changing small-group sessions.

## The Boundaries Groupware kit includes:

### 1 94-minute video

This nine-part video features the wisdom and insight of Dr. Cloud and Dr. Townsend, popular speakers and experts in the integration of Scripture and psychology. Interspersed are helpful real-life vignettes of people struggling to establish and live by godly boundaries.

### 1 Leader's (Revised) Guide*

This comprehensive, user-friendly guide provides all the information you need to lead your group through the nine sessions of this course.

### 1 Participant's (Revised) Guide*

This guide provides valuable notes and practical exercises (small-group discussion starters, independent Bible studies, "Boundary Building" questions, etc.) that will help individuals apply to their lives the principles they learn.

### 1 *Boundaries* hardcover book*

In this longtime best-seller, Dr. Henry Cloud and Dr. John Townsend offer biblically based guidelines for setting healthy boundaries with our parents, spouses, children, friends, coworkers, and even ourselves.

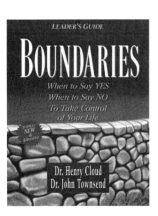

*Boundaries* interactive sessions include:

- What Is a Boundary?
- Understanding Boundaries
- The Laws of Boundaries, Part I
- The Laws of Boundaries, Part II
- Myths About Boundaries
- Boundary Conflicts, Part I
- Boundary Conflicts, Part II
- Boundary Successes, Part I
- Boundary Successes, Part II

*\*Additional copies may be purchased separately*

"Dr. Henry Cloud and Dr. John Townsend have great insight and practical wisdom into the God-given gift of *Boundaries*. As they discuss how to take personal responsibility for and ownership of our lives, they give us hope that we can not just survive but thrive!"

**Josh McDowell** *Author and speaker*

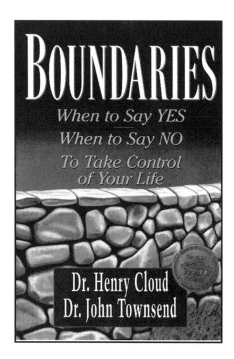
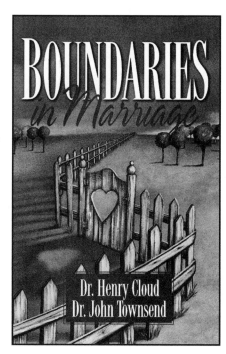

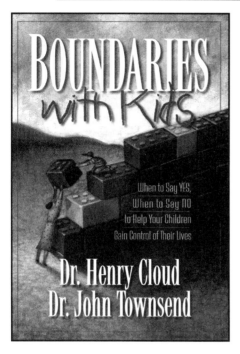

## BOUNDARIES WITH KIDS

Helps parents set boundaries with their children and helps them teach their children the concept of boundaries.

Hardcover 0-310-20035-0
Audio Pages 0-310-59560-6
Workbook 0-310-22349-0

## BOUNDARIES IN DATING

Road map to the kind of enjoyable, rewarding dating that can take you from weekends alone to a lifetime with the soul mate you've longed for.

Softcover 0-310-20034-2
Audio pages 0-310-24055-0
Workbook 0-310-23330-5
Zondervan*Groupware*™ 0-310-23873-0
Leader's Guide 0-310-23874-9
Participant's Guide 0-310-23875-7

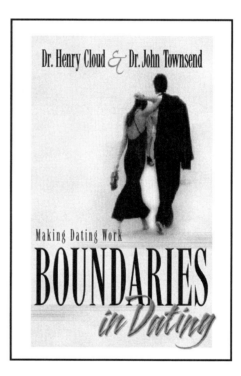

## *Pick up a copy today at your favorite bookstore!*

ZondervanPublishingHouse
*Grand Rapids, Michigan 49530*
http://www.zondervan.com

# Other Great Resources by Dr. Henry Cloud and Dr. John Townsend

## RAISING GREAT KIDS
*A Comprehensive Guide to Parenting with Grace and Truth*

Hardcover 0-310-22569-8
Softcover 0-310-23549-9
Audio Pages 0-310-22572-8
Workbook for Parents of Preschoolers 0-310-22571-X
Workbook for Parents of School-Age Children 0-310-23452-2
Workbook for Parents of Teenagers 0-310-23437-9
Zondervan *Groupware™* for Parents of Preschoolers
0-310-23238-4
Parents of Preschoolers Leader's Guide 0-310-23296-1
Parents of Preschoolers Participant's Guide 0-310-23295-3

## SAFE PEOPLE
*How to Find Relationships That Are Good for You and Avoid Those That Aren't*

Softcover 0-310-21084-4
Mass Market 0-310-49501-6
Audio Pages 0-310-59568-1

## CHANGES THAT HEAL
*How to Understand Your Past to Ensure a Healthier Future*
**Dr. Henry Cloud**

Softcover 0-310-60631-4
Mass Market 0-310-21463-7
Audio Pages 0-310-20567-0
Workbook 0-310-60633-0

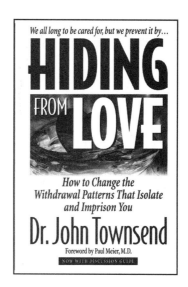

We want to hear from you. Please send your comments about this book to us in care of the address below. Thank you.

ZondervanPublishingHouse
*Grand Rapids, Michigan 49530*
http://www.zondervan.com